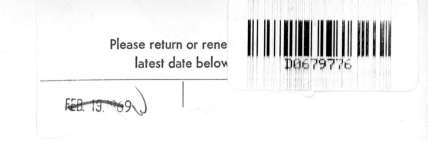

THE REFERENCE SHELF   VOLUME 37   NUMBER 1

FERMENT IN EASTERN EUROPE

EDITED BY
IRWIN ISENBERG

Associate Editor, Foreign Policy Association

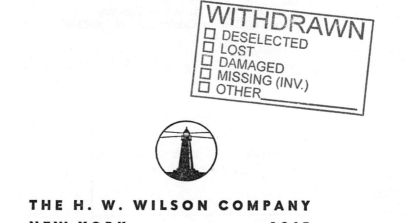

THE H. W. WILSON COMPANY
NEW YORK   1965

THE REFERENCE SHELF

The books in this series contain reprints of articles, excerpts from books, and addresses on current issues, social trends, and other aspects of American life, and occasional surveys of other countries. Six numbers, comprising a volume, are published in each calendar year. One number is a collection of recent speeches on a variety of topics; each of the others, devoted to a single subject, gives background information and discussion from various points of view and concludes with a comprehensive bibliography.

Subscribers to the current volume receive the books as issued. The subscription rate is $12 ($15 foreign) for a volume of six numbers. Single numbers are $3 each.

PREFACE

In the mid-1960's the Communists are still firmly entrenched in Eastern Europe. But their domains are a study in motion and flexibility. Powerful economic, political, and social forces are giving a new look to this part of the Old World. It is a picture with many inconsistent features. Progress contrasts with stagnation, increased liberty wth persistent repression, friendly government approaches to the West with harsh official statements.

The regimes are committed to the building of Communist societies, yet there has been a noticeable weakening of Marxist ideology. Though dictatorship prevails, control has loosened. National differences, long hidden under the veneer of Communist solidarity, are more visible.

Signs of change crop up in many guises. Moscow no longer dictates as much as it persuades: Eastern European Communist leaders indicated, to some extent, their independence from Kremlin control when they voiced reservations about the method used to oust former Soviet Premier Khrushchev in October 1964. Rumania has refused to go along with bloc-wide plans for economic integration. The Polish regime is waging a running battle against the intellectuals, and the intellectuals are fighting back vigorously in their demand for more freedom of expression. Even Bulgaria, long one of the most tightly controlled nations in the Soviet sphere, has loosened up to the point where thousands of political prisoners have been released.

State planning and centralization are under attack. Stress is being put upon the necessity of allowing factory managers more power of decision. The performance of some industrial enterprises is now being judged by whether they make a profit, not by whether they meet their quota in the state plan. Socialized agriculture is plagued by problems and new incentives have been offered to the farmers. The Czechoslovakian economy is in serious difficulty. There is brewing tension between nationality groups in Rumania.

The current ferment stems from many related factors, some of them rooted in national history and temperament. The course of de-Stalinization and the attendant easing of police state methods allowed the people to voice their dissatisfaction. This forced the Communist regimes to grant concessions in order to win tolerance. Khrushchev's policy of peaceful coexistence encouraged the countries of Eastern Europe to open new lines of communication and contact with the West. The Sino-Soviet rift presented an opportunity to gain maneuverability by playing off one Communist giant against the other.

Where does all this leave Eastern Europe? It is still tied to Moscow, but it is also facing westward. Can Eastern Europe be weaned further away from the Kremlin? Should the West offer favorable trade terms to those countries which show signs of independence from Moscow? Should the West even extend appropriate forms of economic aid to help the Communists out of their present difficulties? Or are such measures foolhardy in view of the traditional Communist goals of subversion and conquest? Should our policies rather be to mount pressures in all feasible ways so as to aggravate current troubles, and to grant no help unless substantial concessions are granted in return?

These questions are important because of Eastern Europe's significant role in world affairs. Three times in our century it has played a central part in major events. It was the scene of the assassination of Austrian Archduke Franz Ferdinand, which triggered World War I. It was the victim of Hitler's first military strike in World War II. The cold war flared up as a result of Soviet policies in Eastern Europe. Furthermore, as the world's fourth largest industrial complex, after the United States, Western Europe, and the Soviet Union, Eastern Europe is a major force in the East-West rivalry, and with its more than 120 million people, it is a significant part of the Communist world. What happens in Eastern Europe, therefore, affects the course of world communism and has a crucial bearing on international developments.

This compilation is a brief survey of the changes now taking place. The articles in the first section provide historical background; those in the second and third sections outline political and economic trends and intrabloc relationships. The last section considers past and present United States policy toward Eastern Europe.

The editor wishes to thank the authors and publishers who have generously granted permission to reprint the selections included in this volume.

IRWIN ISENBERG

January 1965

A NOTE TO THE READER

For additional material on East Germany, the reader should consult *The Two Germanies*, edited by Grant S. McClellan and published in 1959 (The Reference Shelf, Volume 31, Number 1).

CONTENTS

	Area in square miles	Population	Capital (population)	Government leader	Average annual output per capita	Chief religion	Per cent of collectivized and state-owned farm-lands	Per cent of literacy
ALBANIA	10,629	1,660,000	Tirana (150,000)	Enver Hoxha	$150	Islam	90	75
BULGARIA	42,796	7,943,000	Sofia (608,000)	Todor Zhivkov	$310	Orthodox	98	85
CZECHO-SLOVAKIA	49,381	13,856,000	Prague (1,005,000)	Antonin Novotny	$990 (approximate)	Roman Catholic	90	98
EAST GERMANY	41,312	17,125,000	East Berlin (1,064,000)	Walter Ulbricht	$990 (approximate)	Lutheran	94	98
HUNGARY	35,918	10,057,000	Budapest (1,830,000)	Janos Kadar	$550	Roman Catholic	96	96
POLAND	120,355	30,324,000	Warsaw (1,300,000)	Wladyslaw Gomulka	$550	Roman Catholic	13	94
RUMANIA	91,584	18,567,000	Bucharest (1,229,000)	Gheorghe Gheorghiu-Dej	$378	Orthodox	96	89
YUGO-SLAVIA	98,766	18,607,000	Belgrade (588,000)	Tito (Josip Broz)	$269	Orthodox & Roman Catholic	10	75

FACTS ON EASTERN EUROPE

Sources: Civic Education Service, Inc., 1733 K St. N.W., Washington, D.C.; Free Europe Committee, Inc., 2 Park Ave., New York, N.Y. 10016; *United Nations Statistical Yearbook 1963, World Almanac 1964.*

EASTERN EUROPE

Wide World Photos

I. HISTORY'S BATTLEFIELD

EDITOR'S INTRODUCTION

The facts of geography have been Eastern Europe's curse for centuries. The northern plains have invited aggression; the southern mountains have prevented unity. In the west were Austria, Prussia, and Germany. These three nations launched many attacks on Eastern Europe and held its people in subservience for long periods. In the south was the Turkish Ottoman Empire. Its rule lasted for more than 400 years in some regions. In the east was, and is, Russia. Caught between these forces, the peoples and nations of Eastern Europe have often been manipulated by the stronger neighboring powers.

In modern times, the geographic vise in which Eastern Europe finds itself has, if anything, tightened. After World War I, the Allies redrew boundary lines to create a number of small, independent states. A system of security alliances created an illusion of safety. In 1938 and 1939, however, Hitler dismembered Czechoslovakia and another grim chapter in Eastern European history began. When the war ended with Hitler destroyed, the Soviet Army was in control of Eastern Europe. This prepared the way for a seizure of power by the Communists.

The articles in this first section recall the tragic past. The section opens with a general account of the region and discusses some of the major themes in its history. Selections on Poland, Czechoslovakia, and the Balkan countries explore the various problems with which these nations had to cope between the wars. Then, as now, the question of Germany was central. Then, as now, poverty was widespread. An excerpt from a British periodical tells the painful story of the 1944 Warsaw uprising against the Germans. The article reveals something of the murderous fury that has regularly wracked Eastern Europe.

This section can provide only a surface look at an extremely complex past. But the articles included here help set the background for an understanding of what happened in this region after World War II—and why.

PAWN OF THE GREAT POWERS [1]

The history of Eastern Europe stretches back through many centuries. Rumania was once an outpost of the Roman Empire. More than a thousand years ago, Bulgaria was a great empire stretching from the Black to the Adriatic Seas. Hungary was a kingdom when explorer Leif Ericson is thought to have discovered America in the year 1000. Renowned universities in Czechoslovakia and Poland flourished before Christopher Columbus was born. The fame of their many illustrious men still lives today.

Copernicus (1473-1543), generally considered the . . . [father of modern astronomy], was born in Poland. The Bohemian Jan Hus, burned at the stake in 1415, was a religious reformer whose teaching profoundly affected European history. Comenius (1592-1670), also a Czech, influenced the educational system of his time. A Polish general, Thaddeus Kosciuszko, fought for the thirteen colonies in the American Revolution. Polish-born Marie Sklodowska Curie (1867-1934), working with her French husband Pierre, discovered one of science's most miraculous tools: radium.

Eastern Europe has given the world such renowned composers as Chopin from Poland, Dvorak and Smetana from Czechoslovakia, Liszt and Bartok from Hungary, and Enesco from Rumania. From Hungary came Ferenc Molnar, the playwright. Statesmen like Tomas and Jan Masaryk and Eduard Benes of Czechoslovakia, and Lajos Kossuth of Hungary, are honored throughout the Western world as fighters for freedom. Eastern Europe has also given millions of new settlers to the United States. Today, American descendants of these East Europeans number more than 15 million.

For all Eastern Europe's great achievements, its history is one of hardship and violence—of war, plunder, poverty, and op-

[1] From *The Soviet Satellites of Eastern Europe*, by Irwin Isenberg, associate editor, Foreign Policy Association. p 9-18. Reprinted by permission from *The Soviet Satellites of Eastern Europe*, by Irwin Isenberg. © 1963 by Scholastic Magazines, Inc. New York.

pression. The many different peoples who inhabit this area have rarely been at peace. There has scarcely been a time when one minority group or another was not persecuted, when some conqueror was not on the march, when armies did not clash on some battlefield.

A tale is told of a meadow in the Serbian region of Yugoslavia, called Kossovo Polye, the "Field of the Black Birds." There, in 1389, troops of several Balkan regions were annihilated by Turkish forces. Today, people say, the red poppies carpeting that field spring from the blood of those fallen soldiers of long ago. If soldiers' blood could make flowers blossom, all Eastern Europe would be in bloom.

Why has such a tragic history plagued Eastern Europe? Why has the region known such confusion and violence? Part of the answer lies in one word: geography.

The Plains: Invitation to Disaster

A broad plain, broken by a few wide swamps and gentle hills, lies over the northern and central sectors of Eastern Europe. The name Poland itself comes from *polya,* which means "field" or "plain." Countless conquering armies have crunched over this vast level land that reaches from the Baltic through Poland to the Carpathian Mountains and other ranges that curve along the Polish-Czech border.

In the thirteenth century, Tatar hordes from Central Asia stormed over this great plain from the east. At about the same time, Germanic knights rode northward to conquer parts of the Baltic coastal lands. Later, Swedish and Polish armies ranged over portions of the plain. Russian armies tramped regularly over the flat earth into Poland. Napoleon crossed it to invade Russia in 1812. Opposing armies sloshed through its mud and swamps in World War I. The Germans pierced it to invade the U.S.S.R. in 1941—and three years later fled back headlong. Too often, people say, the farmer sows grain in the spring and harvests a crop of ruin.

Poland, especially, which lies entirely within this plain, has suffered military tragedies for centuries. Four times—the last in 1939—it was partitioned by the great powers to the east and the west. At one time, between 1795 and 1918, it disappeared from the map, having been swallowed by Austria, Prussia (later a part of Germany), and Russia. Invasions and foreign domination also darken the histories of the Baltic lands of Estonia, Latvia, and Lithuania.

The Mountains: Gateway to Invaders

South of the great plain the land becomes more rugged. The Transylvanian Alps and Carpathian Mountains rise in a great curve through Rumania. The Balkan and Rhodope Mountains separate parts of Bulgaria. Other ranges crisscross Yugoslavia and Albania. Ringed by mountains, most of Hungary is a plain which extends south into Yugoslavia.

The region is watered by many rivers—especially the Vistula of Poland and the majestic Danube, which flows for 1,750 miles past the great cities of Vienna, Budapest, and Belgrade, and between Rumania and Bulgaria toward the Black Sea. These and many other streams flow across the plains and gush through the mountains. They help provide Eastern Europe with systems of irrigation, transport, and water power for industrial and other uses.

Yet land travel was hard in such a region. Towns a few miles apart had little contact with each other, and even less with the outside world. Difficulties of travel, together with the general poverty, made the region the least developed in Europe— and the one most open to conquest by foreign powers. Valleys and mountain passes invited invaders to march in and capture its cities.

Thus the Austrian and Turkish empires, from the northwest and the southeast, found it relatively easy to control large pieces of land in this part of Europe. For centuries the Austrians held Hungary, Czechoslovakia, and parts of Yugoslavia, while the Turks ruled over Bulgaria, Albania, and much of Rumania and

Yugoslavia. Giant Russia stood in the east, ready to seize any occasion to exert its power and extend its realm.

Nationality: A Threat to Peace

Another source of Eastern Europe's violent history lies in its mixture of religions and nationalities. In Yugoslavia for example, Moslem, Roman Catholic, and Eastern Orthodox groups form substantial percentages of the population. (The Orthodox and Roman Catholic religions are alike in many respects, but the Orthodox Church does not recognize the authority of the Roman Catholic Pope.) . . . In one town of 30,000, Uzhgorod, in the Soviet Union [in the Ukraine, but formerly part of Czechoslovakia], a dozen newspapers were once published—each in a different language: Bulgarian, Czech, French, German, Hebrew, Magyar, Polish, Rumanian, Russian, Slovak, Ukrainian, and Yiddish.

Until World War II many Germans and Ukrainians lived in Poland; Poles and Germans on the Baltic Sea; Germans in Czechoslovakia, Hungary, and the Balkans; Bulgarians and Hungarians in Turkey; and Turks in Bulgaria. Large Jewish minorities lived in several East European nations. (Border changes made after World War I, mass killings during World War II, and later transfers of population have altered but not removed minority problems.) Throughout Eastern Europe, such national and religious mixtures led to bickering, blood feuds, and civil war.

Harsh discrimination against minority groups was common. Often they were forbidden to speak their own languages or even to conduct their own schools. Certain jobs and professions were closed to them. Anti-Semitism plagued many lands, especially Rumania, Germany, and Poland. The different peoples of Yugoslavia often battled among themselves. So did the tribes of Albania. Political leaders were frequently assassinated by disgruntled factions.

To make matters worse, many schools in Eastern Europe instilled in their pupils an extreme brand of nationalism. The Poles learned to hate both the Russians and the Germans. Most

Rumanians despised the Bulgarians. Czechs sneered at Hungarians, and Hungarians scorned Rumanians.

Often it was only the great power of old empires that kept the region from collapsing in anarchy. But neither the Hapsburgs, rulers of the Austrian Empire, the Hohenzollerns (whose German Empire included parts of present-day Poland), the Romanovs in Russia, nor the Turks in southeastern Europe could bring lasting harmony to the diverse peoples of their realms. Usually the Turks made no such effort, since the divided, feuding peoples could not effectively challenge their rule.

The plains and mountains of Eastern Europe hold treasures of national wealth. Fertile soil covers large areas, and in normal times the region produces surpluses of food. Wheat, barley, potatoes, rye, oats, corn, and sugar beets are among the chief crops. Tobacco and fruits, including plums from which is made a throat-searing brandy called *slivovits,* grow in the south.

Eastern Europe is also rich in iron ore, coal, lead, zinc, copper, and other minerals. Poland ranks high among the world's coal-producing nations. Europe's most productive oil wells are in Rumania. Yugoslavia is a leading producer of antimony and bauxite, the ore from which aluminum is extracted. Czechoslovakia has important deposits of uranium.

Until recently, however, much of the industrial potential remained untapped. Many East Europeans lived in small towns and villages. Often they worked as farmers, with primitive equipment. Then, as now, their fields produced only a fraction as much as those in Western Europe. . . . Under the old feudal order, a privileged few remained on top; the underprivileged many stayed at the bottom.

The Old Order Crumbles

The end of the great European empires began in the nineteenth century. In 1867 Austria granted limited self-government to Hungary. In 1878 Rumania wrenched itself free from Turkey. . . .

World War I struck a fatal blow to the old order. The Austrian, German, and Russian monarchies were swept away. After the war, the victorious Allies decided to create a new system. They hoped to insure peace and stability by recognizing the independence of nationalities which had freed themselves from the defeated empires. Poland was restored to freedom. Czechoslovakia and Yugoslavia were carved out of the Austro-Hungarian Empire.

The Peace Conference [after World War I] tried to group people of one nationality within the same nation. For example, before World War I the Magyars, or Hungarians, numbered only 50 per cent of the population of Hungary. When the maps were redrawn after the war, the territory of Hungary was reduced and the Magyars numbered 90 per cent of the population. But the peoples of Eastern Europe overlapped so much, and there were so many small pockets of minorities, that no boundaries could separate all the nationalities.

POLAND BETWEEN THE TWO WARS [2]

There was never much doubt among the leaders of the Allied cause during the First World War that the Polish state should be restored. President Woodrow Wilson, in his formulation of the conditions of peace—the so-called "Fourteen Points"—demanded that "an independent Polish state should be erected which should include the territories inhabited by indisputably Polish populations, which should be assured a free and secure access to the sea. . . ." The difficulty was, of course, that the areas "inhabited by indisputably Polish populations" lay within the boundaries of three great empires: the German, Austrian, and Russian. . . .

The new Polish state had necessarily to be carved out of the territory of the three defeated empires, and its extent was a matter for negotiation at the Peace Conference which would end the First World War. . . .

[2] From *Poland Between East and West*, by Norman J. G. Pounds, chairman, department of geography, Indiana University. Van Nostrand. Princeton, N.J. '64. p 62-85. Copyright © 1964 by D. Van Nostrand Company, Inc. Reprinted by permission.

The future boundaries of Poland presented one of the matters of sharpest controversy at the Paris Conference. Woodrow Wilson, feebly supported by the British delegation, claimed that the course of the political boundary should not be allowed at any point to violate the national aspirations of the peoples whom it was to divide. France, on the other hand, consistently struggled to achieve a territorially large and politically strong Poland, which in turn meant a relatively weak Germany. . . .

Wilson had assured the Poles that they should have a "free and secure access to the sea," and this, it was assumed, would take the shape of a corridor of Polish territory reaching down the Vistula valley to the coast of the Baltic Sea, where lay the only significant port within reach of the Polish state, Danzig. By the terms of the peace treaty, Poland was awarded this territory, but the reasons for this decision were not wholly obvious. "Poland needs an access to the sea," wrote C. H. Haskins and R. H. Lord, "but it was not solely because she needed it that she obtained it. The Peace Conference probably would not have satisfied this desire if ethnical reasons had not authorized it to do so. The Conference did not invent the Corridor: it existed already." [*Some Problems of the Peace Conference,* Harvard University Press, Cambridge, Massachusetts, 1920, page 153]

The "Corridor" area coincided very approximately with that region, sometimes known as West Prussia, which lay between Pomerania and East Prussia and had been occupied by the Germans for only a relatively short period before the time of the partitions. It did not become as fully Germanized as either of the territories to west and east, and in 1919 still contained a considerable Polish-speaking population. Poland's claim to the "Corridor" could thus be justified on the Wilsonian argument of the self-determination of nations. It was unfortunate that it was widely assumed that the boundaries were drawn and East Prussia was separated from the rest of Germany merely to give Poland an outlet to the sea. . . .

The prosperity of Danzig . . . had been based on the commerce of its Polish hinterland. Poland was as necessary to Danzig as Danzig was to Poland. Yet about 90 per cent of its population of some 170,000 was German, and proved itself to be aggressively and nationalistically German.

The Danzig problem was never solved, and it proved to be, twenty years later, the pretext for the Second World War. The Poles claimed, and were, of course, supported by the French, that economic necessity should be allowed to override the wishes of the German majority in the city. [British Prime Minister] Lloyd George and Woodrow Wilson were opposed to handing over so many Germans to the untried government of Poland, not so much out of regard for the well-being of the Germans themselves as from fear that they would become again a focus of German intrigue and aggression. In the end there was proposed by Lloyd George and accepted by the Committee of the Conference entrusted with the settlement of the Polish question, the compromise whereby Danzig became a Free City.

For twenty years it retained this status, incorporated into neither Poland nor Germany, though in customs union with the former and sentimentally attached to the latter. The Free City [included territory which] covered an area of only 731 square miles, and its population at the time of the 1929 census was only 407,500. Sovereignty over it was vested in the League of Nations, which appointed its chief executive officer, or high commissioner, who administered the city with the assistance of an elected senate. Danzig had its own currency and postal service.

From the very start there were difficulties between the Polish government and the population of Danzig. In 1920, when Poland was being invaded by the Red Army, war supplies were urgently needed to resist the Soviet attack. These were brought by ship from France and Great Britain, and came into Poland by the only available entry, the port of Danzig. It was at this critical moment that German dock workers refused to unload ships bearing war supplies for Poland. The crisis was weathered, but the Poles did not forget their temporary embarrassment. They determined that for the future they would give no such hostage to the good will of the Danzig Germans, and they embarked on the construction of an alternate and, as events were to show, rival port at Gdynia, fourteen miles along the coast to the north-northwest of Danzig.

What may have been only a temporary intransigence ripened into a mortal hatred, as the port of Gdynia threatened the economic foundations of the port of Danzig. National Socialism, founded on hatred and resentment, was fed by economic depression; and Danzig, though outside the boundary of Hitler's Reich, became one of the earliest cities to raise its hand in a Nazi salute to the German dictator. . . .

Poland, 1922-1939

By 1922, the boundaries of the new Poland were finally established and accepted. They included an area of 146,821 square miles, with a population of 27.1 million. Poland became one of the largest countries in Europe, exceeded in area only by Germany, France, Spain, and Sweden, and in population by Germany, France, Italy, and the United Kingdom.

The conditions which had allowed Poland to be reborn on so generous a scale deserve to be examined. The Poland of 1923 had boundaries in the west that were approximately the same as those existing before the partitions, and in the east they differed little from the line established after the second partition of 1793. The shape and size of Poland tended to reflect the balance of power in Europe between Germany to the west and Russia to the east. During the period of her greatest territorial extent, that is, during the century preceding the wars of the late seventeenth century, Germany was politically divided and torn by civil war, and the Russian Empire weak and ineffective. As soon as either or both of these powers could rouse themselves and organize their resources, the days of an extensive Polish empire were numbered. . . .

In 1918 both the German and the Russian empires were defeated, and Poland was enabled to reappear on the political map of Europe and to expand at the expense of both. The wartime Allies claimed, through their Council of Ambassadors and the League of Nations, some control over the extension of the boundaries of Poland. They were able directly to control the delimitation of the western boundaries, because it was they who wrote the treaties of Versailles and Saint-Germain, which ended the war with Germany and Austria. In the drawing of these western boundaries, the Wilsonian principle of the self-determination of national groups was applied, and the statesmen who met in Paris and at the many subsequent meetings to clarify or confirm the interpretation of the treaties made a fair and generally successful attempt to shape the boundaries to the expressed desires of the peoples whom they were to separate.

As far as the eastern boundaries were concerned, the Allied statesmen could advise and recommend, but they had no power to enforce their decisions. Their recommendations here too followed the Wilsonian line. The most important of them, the Line of December 8, 1919, and the Foch Line [named for French Marshal Ferdinand Foch] were honest and reasonable attempts to separate areas predominantly Polish from those in which a majority appeared to be non-Polish. The Foch Line, by and large, was accepted because it suited the policy of the Poles to follow it. The December 8 Line was ignored, and the Polish armies [in a campaign against the Soviet Union] went on to conquer an empire to which they had an historical claim, but no justification on any Wilsonian principle. Historical claims—and, in the context of Central and Eastern Europe, this means claims based upon medieval and feudal pretensions—have no relevance to the twentieth century. It is one of the tragedies of Europe that peoples of Central and Eastern Europe, with long historical memories and little historical sense, cling so obstinately to these illusions of vanished grandeur. The map of Poland was later to be reshaped according to principles that were neither Wilsonian nor feudal.

Thus it was that Poland came to embrace in the eastern third of the state a mixed population of some 10 million (according to the census of 1931)—about a third of its total population—that was Polish in neither language nor sympathy. It was made up of Lithuanians, Russians, White Russians, and Ukrainians, with a sprinkling of Jews, who also were not thought of and did not consider themselves to be Poles.

It became clear as, in the spring of 1919, the treaties of peace were slowly taking shape, that however fairly and impartially boundaries were delimited, the confused ethnic pattern of much of Central and Eastern Europe was such that ethnic minorities could only be reduced and not eliminated. A Minorities Treaty was drawn up by the Paris Conference and offered to Poland for signature in June, 1919. By the terms of this treaty, which became a model for all other minority treaties, Poland undertook to guarantee to all its citizens complete protection of life and liberty, freedom of religion, the same civil and political rights, and the right to use non-Polish languages privately, in publications, and in the courts of law, without any distinction of birth, nationality, language, or race.

It would have been difficult under any conditions to implement the Minorities Treaty in Poland, and particularly difficult under the social conditions which existed in the Polish East. Here was to be found a poor and predominantly non-Polish peasantry, living on estates owned generally by Poles, and exploited by petty traders who were usually Jewish. By and large the town population was made up of Poles and Jews; the rural population, of White Russians and Ukrainians. The Poles were almost invariably Roman Catholic; their Russian subjects, either members of the Orthodox or of the Uniate church. Any economic conflict within this area— and there was abundant scope for such to develop—could, and usually did, become a communal dispute between Poles and non-Poles.

For much of the interwar period there was latent or open conflict in eastern Poland. Commonly it assumed the shape of a reign of terror by the Polish land-owning and middle classes and of retaliatory burning of hay-ricks and farms by their dependent White Russian and Ukrainian tenants.

The mechanism of democratic government, which should have been able to heal these rifts within the body politic by providing a forum where minorities could air their grievances, worked only feebly and spasmodically in Poland. Its citizens had lived too long in the closed societies of the three empires to understand the workings of an open society. Political parties proliferated, and with their increase in numbers came a refusal to compromise, even when the future of the country and its economy were at stake. The extreme nationalists, the peasants, the socialists, the minorities—each formed separate parties with conflicting interests. The government and civil service lacked experience; credit was weak, and inflation rampant. . . .

Foreign Policy of Poland, 1919-1939

The foreign policy of Poland was determined in advance by the circumstances which had allowed Poland to emerge again on the European map: to prevent the revival of those forces—the nationalism and power of Germany and the Soviet Union—to whose defeat Poland owed its existence. From the start Poland's closest ally was France, in part because of the sentimental ties which had long held the Poles and the French together, in part because France shared the same dangers as Poland. To the French, Germany was the greater source of danger, while to most Poles the Soviet Union presented the major threat. Nevertheless, the French were willing and eager to support Poland as part of a *cordon sanitaire,* a bulwark against the westward extension of Soviet communism. Thus it was the French who saw the greatest advantage in the increase of the territorial extent and the economic power of Poland. It was French arms that helped to turn the tide of Russian advance on the Vistula in 1920, and it was the French Premier, Alexandre Millerand, who invited Pilsudski [chief of the Polish state] to come to Paris, and his foreign minister, Aristide Briand, who negotiated the Franco-Polish treaty of mutual help and protection in February, 1921. Soon afterwards Poland entered into similar treaties with Rumania, exposed like herself to Soviet infiltration and attack, and Czechoslovakia.

France was the architect of a system of alliances, both between herself and the countries of East-Central Europe and between these countries themselves, and it was France who did most to give these alliances a political value by assisting in the economic and military development of her allies. . . .

For several years longer, Poland continued to put her trust in the alliance with France. Germany had in the meanwhile recovered from her defeat. Armaments were being accumulated, openly or illicitly, and the restrictions imposed by the Treaty of Versailles either evaded or renounced. At the same time, the Soviet Union was beginning to organize its immense potential. The adequacy of the French alliance to preserve the integrity of Poland in this newly developing power balance began to be questioned, especially as it became more and more clear that France was incapable of bringing material aid to Poland.

Jozef Beck became Polish foreign minister in 1932. His policy, poorly conceived and incompetently pursued, was to play Germany off against the Soviet Union, as if Poland had the power and resources to shape the balance of Central and Eastern Europe. A nonaggression pact with the Soviet Union in 1932 was followed by a similar pact with Nazi Germany in 1934. Neither pact served to protect Poland, and Beck should have known that differences in political ideology and interest had never prevented Russia from collaborating with Prussia or the Soviet Union with Germany.

While reaffirming repeatedly his loyalty to the nonaggression pact with Poland, Hitler did not cease to enlarge upon the evils done to Germany by the settlement of Paris. In particular he denounced the existence of the "Corridor" and of the Free City of Danzig. In March 1939, Hitler occupied what was left of Czechoslovakia. Great Britain and France, who had stood helplessly by while Czechoslovakia was destroyed piecemeal, now rushed to give guarantees and promises of aid to Poland, which they were no more competent to assist than they had been to aid Czechoslovakia. All that this treaty meant was that if Germany attacked Poland she would be faced also with a war in the west against Great Britain and France.

Even so, the threatened German assault on Poland was slow in coming, and it had to wait until Hitler had eliminated all danger of Soviet interference. There had been so many precedents for a Russian-German rapprochement that the Molotov-Ribbentrop pact of August 21, 1939, ought perhaps to have been anticipated. It was not. The two totalitarian dictatorships concluded a pact of nonaggression, and the Soviet Union undertook to remain neutral in any contest between Germany and Poland. A further agreement, not disclosed at the time though made clear within a month, provided for the fourth partition of Poland. . . .

On September 1, 1939, the German armies invaded Poland. The declaration of war on Germany by Great Britain and France three days later made little difference to the fate of Poland, and by September 8, German armies were in the suburbs of Warsaw. By the middle of the month the Polish armies had been broken up into small pockets of resistance. Then, on September 17, Soviet troops advanced across the eastern boundary of Poland and up to the partition line already agreed upon by Molotov and Ribbentrop in their secret protocol. Although the last Polish resistance was not overcome until well into October, the Russian invasion marked the effective defeat of the Poles. For six years their country lay partitioned and occupied. Its resources were despoiled and its manpower decimated. Yet out of its ashes a new Poland was reborn, tailored to fit yet another balance of political forces in Europe.

TRAGEDY IN CZECHOSLOVAKIA [3]

Most of Czechoslovakia's 13.8 million people live in the western two thirds of the country. There lie Bohemia and Moravia, the most highly developed industrial regions. East of them is Slovakia.

The Czechs and Slovaks are Slavs, or descendants of a people who migrated into Central Europe about the seventh century. In the tenth century, the Hungarians occupied Slovakia, and held it until 1918. But the land of the Czechs grew into a powerful kingdom. At one time it extended from the Oder River in Germany to the Adriatic Sea.

Under King Charles IV (1316-1378), Prague became a center of European civilization. Its Charles University, founded in 1348,

[3] From *The Soviet Satellites of Eastern Europe*, by Irwin Isenberg, associate editor, Foreign Policy Association. p 56-61. Reprinted by permission from *The Soviet Satellites of Eastern Europe*, by Irwin Isenberg. © 1963 by Scholastic Magazines, Inc. New York.

was a mecca for scholars. Many cathedrals and palaces that grace Prague today date from that period. Part of Hradcany Palace, the Czech "White House," were built at that time.

A fateful event for Bohemia occurred in 1526, when its nobles elected as their king the ruler of neighboring Austria, Archduke Ferdinand of Hapsburg. The Hapsburg dynasty dominated Bohemia from that day until 1918. . . .

With the outbreak of World War I, [Tomas] Masaryk [a prominent Czech professor] and his young colleague, Eduard Benes, fled . . . [to America and organized] a movement for an independent Czech nation. Masaryk and Benes won the support of President Woodrow Wilson and the Allies.

Though Bohemia-Moravia, as part of the Austrian Empire, was at war with the Allies, thousands of Czechs fled to the west to fight the Hapsburgs. In 1918, when Austrian collapse was near, Bohemian and Slovak leaders, inspired by Masaryk, met in Pittsburgh, Pennsylvania. They agreed to form a new nation, made up of Bohemia, Moravia, and Slovakia, which was to be detached from Hungary by the peace settlement. Masaryk became president of the new republic, Benes its foreign minister.

A smaller area within the new Czechoslovakia was Ruthenia [part of the Ukraine], also called Sub-Carpathian Russia. An agricultural region at the eastern tip of the country, it was inhabited by about 900,000 people and had been ruled by Hungary.

In the interwar period, Czechoslovakia built the framework for a stable democracy. It adopted a constitution based largely on those of the United States and France. The great estates of the [Austrian and Hungarian] nobles were distributed to the peasants.

The nation made rapid economic strides. In Ruthenia, roads were built for the first time in five hundred years. Large quantities of tools and machinery were exported. Czech craftsmen won a reputation for quality workmanship that endures today. Moscow women, it is said, would stand in line for hours to buy a pair of Czech-made shoes.

But the Czechs faced serious political problems. Hungary demanded the return of those parts of Slovakia inhabited chiefly by Hungarians. Slovakia insisted on more self-rule within the national government. . . . .

Trouble in the Sudetenland

In the 1930's, the menace of Nazi Germany rose in the West. Adolf Hitler denounced Czechoslovakia for "oppressing" the Sudetenland Germans, who had long lived in the Sudeten Mountain border regions. These Germans, it is true, had been denied some opportunities. They could not hold certain civil-service jobs. But they did not suffer from widespread oppression.

Czechoslovakia negotiated a mutual security pact with the Soviet Union in 1935. This reinforced a pact signed with France in 1924. Czech leaders hoped that these treaties would protect the nation from Hitler. As German pressures grew, [the elderly] Masaryk resigned [in 1935] and Benes became the new Czech president. The tension reached a peak when Hitler, proclaiming himself protector of all Sudetenland Germans, demanded that the region be ceded to Germany.

The Czechs protested. Germany had no legal claim to the Sudetenland. Loss of the area would deprive Czechoslovakia of an economically valuable region and strip it of a mountain ring forming a natural line of defense.

Hitler's demands opened one of the darkest pages in Western diplomacy. In September 1938, a conference took place in Munich, attended by the prime ministers of Germany, Italy, Britain, and France. Czechoslovakia, whose existence was at stake, was not even represented at this meeting. England and France, afraid of a major war, weakly agreed to surrender the Sudetenland to Hitler.

Czechs received the news in stunned disbelief. Many have never forgiven the West for this appeasement, which was based on the vain hope of satisfying Hitler's lust for more land, or "living space" for Germany, as he called it. When British Prime Minister Chamberlain returned from Munich, he announced that he "brought back peace in our time." Chamberlain's "peace" lasted less than one year.

In the eleven months between the Munich settlement and the outbreak of World War II on September 1, 1939, Hitler's armies goose-stepped into all Bohemia and Moravia. Slovakia was allowed to proclaim its "independence," and became a German puppet. Hungary seized part of Ruthenia [Ukraine]. Poland, too, took a piece of Czech territory. Czechoslovakia was completely dismembered.

When Hitler made new territorial demands in 1939, this time on Poland, the West's backbone stiffened. Unable to seize more land without a conflict, he invaded Poland and plunged Europe into war.

THE BALKAN ECONOMY [4]

In analyzing the transformation of the Balkan countries since their independence, it should be pointed out that the social and economic conditions within the decaying Ottoman Empire set the bench marks for the independent development and economic progress of the three countries [Albania, Bulgaria, and Yugoslavia] under discussion. While the three countries show many joint characteristics and have had many periods of similar social and economic development—for example, their large agricultural population, their undeveloped resources, and their dependence upon foreign capital for the development of their economy—they differ in a number of important aspects, particularly in size, population, and the availability of raw materials. They also achieved control of their political destinies at widely differing times. Serbia [now part of Yugoslavia] was the first to gain autonomy (1830) and later full independence (1878) from Turkish rule, followed by Bulgaria (1908) and only after World War I by Albania. Progress was interrupted repeatedly by wars and domestic upheavals. While Serbia was greatly enlarged and

[4] From *The Balkans in Transition*, by George W. Hoffman, professor of geography, University of Texas. Van Nostrand. Princeton, N.J. '63. p 72-80. Copyright © 1963 by D. Van Nostrand Company, Inc. Reprinted by permission.

enriched in these wars by the acquisition of additional territory, manpower, and raw materials, Bulgaria, being on the losing side [in the Balkan wars and World War I], remained small in size and population, with only limited economic progress. Political unrest also was common to all three countries before World War II.

All three Balkan countries—and for that matter, neighboring Greece and Rumania too—had a common social and economic base and a common identity of purpose when their hard-won autonomy within the Ottoman Empire, and later their independence, began. The common base was determined by the joint experience of several hundred years under Ottoman control. It was expressed in their great poverty, the high percentage of illiteracy among the masses, a population dependent upon income derived largely from agriculture (80-90 per cent), a large surplus agricultural labor force (35-50 per cent), and very low productivity. The poverty of a large percentage of the peasants arose in part from the dwarf and divided landholdings that made it simply impossible to increase productivity by using improved techniques. These small, divided holdings were located mainly in Bulgaria, northern Albania, Montenegro [in Yugoslavia] and Serbia, while in the Austro-Hungarian region that later became [part of] Yugoslavia, larger estates worked by landless peasants prevailed until 1918. The agrarian reform after World War I also created small holdings there. Peasants produced cereal crops mainly, and even the more fertile regions could not easily distribute their surpluses to other parts of the same country because of the deplorable condition of transportation. Obviously, the central problem for the governments in the Balkans was how to combat the agrarian overpopulation that was so closely connected with low productivity and the low standard of living.

Industrialization was relatively unknown in any of the Balkan countries in the nineteenth century. It was confined to those parts under Austrian control, especially Slovenia [now in Yugoslavia]. Handicrafts were substantial in Bulgaria. The considerable wealth of mineral resources (gold, silver, iron, and copper), especially in southern Serbia, while already exploited during the medieval Great Serbian Empire, was largely neglected during the Ottoman period. Effective exploitation did not commence until the interwar years, when foreign capital made it possible. Albanian and Bulgarian mineral resources were small compared with those of Serbia and especially later Yugoslavia. With the large agrarian population, urban settlements were few in number and very small. Belgrade [the future capital of Yugoslavia], for example, had only 70,000 inhabitants by the turn of the century. The rural population of Bulgaria in 1880 amounted to 83 per cent of the whole population, and it remained unchanged until World War II.

Independence for the three countries, won after hard and prolonged fighting, meant a sudden change in existing social and economic conditions. These countries withdrew from the cloak of the Ottoman Empire, which gave protection to their local self-government, often based on old patriarchal forms and customs, and rushed into the forms of parliamentary democracy, which was looked upon with great hope. Inexperience was quickly shown, and Western constitutional practices collapsed at an early stage (Albania 1927, Yugoslavia 1929, Bulgaria 1934). The citizens of the newly independent countries had little feeling of responsibility toward the organs of the state. Corruption, so common in the Turkish state, and animosity toward state administrative organs generally continued to be widespread. Each of the newly independent countries gave high priority to modern armies and the fulfillment of ill-defined material aspirations. Questions of nationalism outweighed economic consideration. At the same time, foreign influence rapidly increased, and with it Great Power rivalries in each of the Balkan countries. . . .

The interwar years were characterized by repeated efforts by the governments to solve the agricultural problem. Roughly 80 per cent of the labor force in Yugoslavia and Bulgaria and even more in Albania were still connected with agriculture. . . . A comprehensive land reform was initiated in the Yugoslav sections of the former Austro-Hungarian monarchy, especially the Vojvodina, which had large estates. Albania remained a tribal society for most of the interwar years, and only 16 per cent of the total area was arable. . . .

The main hope of the governments for an expanding economy during the interwar years was industrialization with the help of state intervention, heavily depending upon foreign capital and protectionist policies. Nationalistic policies of the worst type were especially strong in Yugoslavia. These were expressed in discrimination against former contacts with Viennese banking institutions by Croatian, Hungarian, or German business. The state also confiscated and ruined many well-managed business enterprises in the hands of minorities. The borrowing of foreign capital increased, resulting in greatly increased indebtedness, increased taxation, and inflation. Self-sufficiency was further accelerated by the great depression of the 1930's, which brought increased state control, declining revenue, and a general lowering of income. Domestic expenditures were cut, and only army expenditures remained high or were increased. For Bulgaria, for example, military appropriations amounted to approximately 33 per cent of the ordinary budget. Foreign trade also declined. The total trade turnover of Bulgaria between 1929 and 1934 fell from $105 million to $34 million, and that of Yugoslavia fell from $270 to $85 million. Only Albania was in a somewhat better position with Italy guaranteeing to buy the limited output of crude oil, bitumen, chrome ore, and timber. Still, exports covered only one fifth of the imports.

On the whole, government policies with regard to increased industrialization and mining showed satisfactory progress. The net output of industrial products, according to national statistics, increased 32 per cent in Yugoslavia, 143 per cent in Bulgaria, and 50 per cent in Albania (based on 1938 or 1939 prices) between 1927 and 1939. In Yugoslavia between 1919 and 1939, production of coal increased strikingly, from 2.2 million to 7 million tons and output of metallic ores rose from 70,000 to 3.2 million tons. Foreign capital investments in Yugoslavia accounted for 46 per cent of the total investments in industry, with the state contributing most of the remainder. The state owned many mines, 40 per cent of the forest area, and 25 per cent of the coal output;

it also had a monopoly on tobacco, silk, and salt. Lack of capital certainly prevented a more rapid development of the economy. Transportation within the country was deplorable and often prevented the exploitation of important deposits. Only international lines were modernized. In Bulgaria, 48 per cent of all corporate capital was foreign. In industry and mining, foreign capital amounted to 24 per cent.

The reliance on such a high percentage of foreign capital, especially in Yugoslavia, meant emphasis on exploitation of minerals that were in great demand in foreign countries. But the financing of domestic industries using local metals was not in the interest of the foreign investors. Finished metals had to be imported. The fact that only 2 per cent of Yugoslavia's national income in 1939 was derived from mineral resources is indicative of the minor impact of this exploitation on the total economy. The total contribution of industry to the national income of Yugoslavia averaged 23 per cent during the interwar period. It averaged 18 per cent in Bulgaria. Albania had no industrial production of importance in the interwar years.

The economic and social progress of the Balkan countries was slow during the interwar years. This sluggishness was in part due to the devastating effects of the depression, which are so clearly illustrated by the low per capita income in 1939 (based on gold dollars of pre-1933)—$30 for Bulgaria, $70 for Yugoslavia, and $25 for Albania. In terms of purchasing power, real income per person was perhaps one fourth to one fifth that of France or the British Isles. The density of the farm population per hundred hectares (250 acres) of cultivated land was still high—103 in Yugoslavia, 107 in Bulgaria, and 97 in Albania. Great differences in the general standard of living and per capital income, between the more advanced parts of Yugoslavia (Slovenia and parts of Croatia) and the backward regions (Montenegro, Macedonia, parts of Serbia) still remained. Slovenia, with only one fifth of the population of Serbia, or somewhat larger than that of Macedonia, contributed twice as much as Serbia to the national budget and four times as much as Macedonia. The heart of Yugoslavia, Bosnia and Herzegovina, remained primitive, and its rich minerals were untapped The percentage of the population depending upon agriculture for their principal income had scarcely been changed in the interwar years; it decreased only from 79 per cent in 1921 to 75 per cent in 1939 in Yugoslavia and remained at 80 per cent in Bulgaria and 90 per cent in Albania. Peasants were frequently caught in the price squeeze between industrial and agricultural prices, and competition from overseas often produced large surpluses. The agrarian problem at the outbreak of World War II remained the most serious social and economic problem of the three Balkan countries.

THE WARSAW RISING [5]

July 1944 was a hot month in Warsaw, but few people were paying attention to the weather. With fascination and pleasure we watched unmistakable signs of the German retreat before the Soviet Army. Long columns of soldiers passed through the city day and night. We heard the sound of heavy artillery clearly to the east, across the Vistula. Soviet airplanes occasionally flew over the city. The Germans were in a jumpy, ugly mood, sniffing sabotage everywhere.

The underground Home Army, perhaps forty thousand strong in Warsaw, was mobilized for some sort of action. I and the friends who had joined with me the year before had formed a platoon of seventeen- and eighteen-year-olds. Our motives were simple; we were eager to show our hatred of the Germans, and we did not want to sit and wait for the Russians to liberate us. Many of us also resented the fact that the Communist shadow government had just been set up in Lublin behind the Russian lines. We regarded the Polish exile government in London as legitimate and were willing to show our loyalty to it.

By the end of July we realized an uprising was imment. On August 1, at about noon, the news came: it was to be that afternoon. I rushed home to snatch some food and change. My parents, who knew I was in the Home Army, sensed something

[5] From article by Zbigniew Pelczynski, lecturer in politics at Oxford University. *The Listener*. 72:577-9. O. 15, '64. Reprinted by permission.

was up. I kissed my mother as I was leaving. It almost gave me away; she looked at me sharply and asked anxiously: "You're coming back tonight as usual, aren't you?" As I blandly lied to her, I was sure we were parting only for a few days; in fact, I didn't see my family again for over twelve years.

I jumped on a crowded tram going to Mokotow, a residential quarter on the southern outskirts of Warsaw where my unit was to assemble. I stood on the rear platform, almost next to a couple of S.S. men, terribly self-conscious of my bulging jacket. I had been given six British hand grenades to carry, and I had simply stuffed them in my pockets. I got off at the same stop as the Germans, who were heading for a large building, once a secondary school and now a heavily guarded and fortified barracks; my destination was a small private house only a block or so away.

The platoon were there in full strength. I was told to lie down on the floor, like the others, and keep still and silent. It was about two o'clock. An hour, two hours, went by. Somewhere in the distance there was a burst of rifle shots. Machine-gun fire started. We still waited. Half-past four, five; someone knocked on the door. The platoon commander came back and said: "This is it, boys. Get up." We filed into a small park nearby. Our commander took out a pistol and stuck it into a leather belt which he wore over his jacket. It was a splendidly symbolic gesture: it meant we were emerging from the underground, becoming insurgents instead of conspirators. But where were *our* arms? A pretty blonde girl came along with a bundle of red-and-white armbands and we were told to put them on. Under some international convention they were supposed to give us the status of soldiers and put us under the protection of the rules of war. In fact, the Germans did not pay the slightest attention to the armbands and shot all prisoners as "bandits." Only much later, after the British threatened reprisals, did the Wehrmacht change their policy. But not the S.S.: always a law unto themselves, they went on killing prisoners to the end. As we waited for arms, the park filled with young men from other platoons of our company. At last a taxi with a red-and-white flag . . . drove up and various weapons were unloaded. We eyed them with greed and disappointment as we realized they had to be divided among three platoons. Our ration was one submachine gun and five rifles, plus ammunition and some hand grenades, enough to arm exactly half the men. For the rest, that night was a terrible anticlimax—there was nothing for them to do.

The lucky half of the company very soon went into action against the fortified S.S. barracks. Two or three times the Poles tried an assault but they were repelled by heavy German fire. At dawn our units withdrew, and we began preparing for a German counterattack. It was a disappointment, but news from other sectors of Mokotow and the rest of Warsaw was more encouraging. Large areas of the city had been cleared of the enemy. The next step was for the rebel forces to link up with each other. The Germans were trying to keep them split by holding on to key buildings and streets until reinforcements could be sent in.

The first victims of the rising were the Polish civilians left behind the German lines. They were being expelled from Warsaw, their homes looted. Men, especially young ones, were executed by the hundred. Incredible atrocities happened only a few yards from our positions. Not far from us there was a house of Jesuit fathers, well known during the occupation for sermons with a political and patriotic slant. It was surrounded by S.S. men who drove all the residents into a cellar and massacred them with machine guns.

On our side, men and women who had not been in the underground before now joined us, and young boys—sometimes no older than twelve or thirteen—begged to be taken on as couriers and orderlies. One of the jobs they did was to act as postmen, delivering letters from one quarter to another through the sewers. The Home Army actually issued its own stamps during the rising. It was one of the things that gave us an illusion of independence. We rather reveled in this illusion. Placards with patriotic manifestos and orders from military and civil authorities mushroomed overnight. Dozens of newspapers and periodicals began to come out regularly, and a radio station controlled by insurgents started broadcasts. Polish flags and eagles replaced German flags and swastikas. Streets and squares had old names restored and all inscriptions in German were painted over. . . .

Bombing became a nuisance in the second half of August. It was the work of three dive bombers. They took off from an airfield near Mokotow early in the morning, disposed of their load, reloaded, and returned with new bombs half an hour later with deadly regularity, for about twelve hours a day. We had no defense against them. One just sheltered somewhere when the Stukas appeared and hoped for the best. One afternoon I was walking to a hospital in search of my missing younger brother. The three planes appeared over the district, so I rushed into the basement of a large, solid-looking house where a lot of other people—many of them women and children—were sheltering. There was a roar of engines, a moment's silence, and then a crash of collapsing walls. We were all buried under three floors of rubble. I was saved from death by two strong beams which had shielded me from falling masonry. A rescue party dug me out after about three hours but there were hardly any other survivors. I was taken to an improvised hospital, in the basement of another house, and kept there for a couple of weeks.

When I joined my unit again I found them in a very different mood. The Germans had managed to spare some tanks and troops from the Russian front and were beginning to put pressure on us. Hopes of massive Western aid from the air had faded. There were many small night drops of arms and ammunition by Allied planes stationed in northern Italy, and one large American day drop—which unfortunately benefited the Germans more than it did us. There was talk of capitulation, and apparently tentative negotiations began. Then on September 11 the Soviet Army reached the outskirts of Warsaw and occupied the district lying to the east of the Vistula. Our hopes soared again. Help from the Russians now seemed a virtual certainty. People suddenly reappeared in the streets in an upsurge of jubilation. For several days bridges were kept on the Polish side of the Vistula to make the crossing easier for the Russians. But, after tremendous losses, the strip of land had to be abandoned. It looked as if the Russians were not interested in saving the uprising from defeat, and this I realized afterwards was true. For many of our leaders, the uprising was a purely political gamble. They hoped, by seizing control of Warsaw, to impress people with their strength and to force the Russians to negotiate with the Polish exile government in London. So it was not surprising the Russians found it convenient to let the Germans crush us.

One quarter after another was falling to the Germans. The bombing was succeeded by shelling from huge guns, heavy mortars, and, worst of all, rockets which ripped whole walls off buildings. Cellars overflowed with the wounded, and with women and children. Water became very scarce and strictly rationed; bread, meat, and fats disappeared, and in the end our daily meal was reduced to one bowl of tasteless gruel. We could scrounge fresh vegetables from allotment fields in no-man's-land but only by organizing armed expeditions at night. One risked one's life for a sack of potatoes, tomatoes, or runner beans. Hunger was driving people to eat horses, dogs, and cats. Eventually the Germans allowed civilians to pass through their lines if they wanted to leave Warsaw, and many took advantage of this.

Towards the end of September the Germans began their attack on Mokotow. On a Sunday morning a barrage of bombs, shells, and rockets broke over the district. The softening-up process went on all day. When it got dark the Germans went into action. The same night, part of my company was sent off to the rear to strengthen the Polish defenses. We stayed there three days, desperately defending one house after another, but we were pushed back all the time. In this short time half the men were killed or badly wounded. Now we held less than a square mile of Mokotow and were encircled by tanks and troops. We could not last more than a few hours. Our troops were to be evacuated that night through the sewers to the last central district of Warsaw in Polish hands.

The next twelve hours were for me the most harrowing period of the uprising. . . . At 3 A.M. I found a long queue of soldiers in front of a manhole—the entrance to a sewer. Somebody gave me a German submachine gun, twenty bullets, and two bottles of vodka to carry. The queue moved forward with agonizing slowness. At last, after three hours, our turn came. We crawled down and then along a low tunnel to the main sewer which was perhaps ten feet high and five wide. Here was another queue. In darkness and silence, one arm on the shoulder of the man in front, up to the knees in stinking muddy liquid, we waded slowly forward trying not to splash or slip. From time to time we could hear tanks rolling above and snatches of German conversation. Suddenly the news flashed down the line: "No way through. All passages blocked by the Germans." Chaos followed, since the men in front began turning back while those behind pressed forward, deaf to all warnings. Suddenly there was a blast of air, and a strong smell which caused a panic. The line broke, units split, the wounded began to go under, screaming and shouting broke out: "They're flooding us!" "Gas! Can you smell gas?" "Back to Mokotow!"

I and two friends—all that remained of my unit—managed to push our way back. Behind us there was another explosion, and then a third, much nearer. The Germans had realized the sewer was full of men. We clung to the sticky, smooth-rounded wall of the sewer waiting for another explosion. Seconds passed, then minutes. Nothing happened. Our nerves could not stand it any longer. We chucked all our weapons away, and made for the nearest manhole. Someone climbed up and cried in broken German: *"Deutsche Soldaten! Nicht schiessen! Hier Polnische Kameraden!"* The Germans roared with laughter and shouted: *"Raus!"* The cover of the manhole was lifted, and one by one a small group of us emerged, hands up, blinking in the sunshine. The soldiers, thank God, were from the Wehrmacht. We were searched, relieved of watches and money, and marched off under guard to a small square in the vicinity of the same park where we had assembled on August 1.

The center capitulated a few days later, and on October 3 the rest of the insurgents began captivity. They joined us in a transit camp near Warsaw from which, in crowded goods trains, we were dispatched to prisoner-of-war camps all over Germany. Then the remaining civilians were forced to leave to leave the city and herded into camps; many ended up in Auschwitz or other concentration camps. Warsaw became a ghost city, wholly deserted except for demolition squads which in the usual German systematic way proceeded to blow up all buildings still left standing. Just before they finished, their work was interrupted by the massive Soviet offensive on January 11, 1945. The same day Warsaw was occupied by the Red Army. But there were no cheers, no flowers, no gratitude for the victors, nobody to be liberated, nothing but ruins and a few deserted buildings.

II. THE SOVIET BLOC—
FROM STALIN TO KHRUSHCHEV

EDITOR'S INTRODUCTION

The period since the end of World War II has been an eventful one for Eastern Europe. By 1948, when Czechoslovakia slipped behind the Iron Curtain as a result of a bloodless coup, the entire region was in Communist hands. The apparatus of modern totalitarianism operated in full measure throughout Eastern Europe until the death of Stalin in 1953. Thereafter, conditions eased in some of the satellites. Despite the relative improvement, 1956 brought rebellion in Poland and Hungary.

It fell to Khrushchev to try to bring some degree of stability and unity to a bloc which had fallen into such a state of disarray in so few years. His efforts met with mixed success; there were no more outright rebellions, yet bloc unity was probably more tenuous at the end of his reign than at the beginning. In fact, the growing disunity within the Soviet bloc may have been partially responsible for the ouster of Khrushchev.

This three-part section covers the years from the end of the war until the end of Khrushchev's rule. The first article, taken from a Foreign Policy Association Headline Series pamphlet, retells the tale of the Communist seizure of power. An excerpt from a book by Hugh Seton-Watson sketches the major developments during the Stalinist era. A subsequent selection speaks of Khrushchev's de-Stalinization speech and its effect on the satellites. The next piece, taken from a UN report, portrays the early stages of the Hungarian revolution and sums up the findings of the world organization on the uprising.

The next part of this section discusses, from various vantage points, events after 1956. It was a time of reconstruction, of attempts to patch up the damage that had been done. One article reviews Khrushchev's efforts in this sphere. Other articles focus on bloc political and economic affairs and on the pace of de-Stalinization in the countries of the bloc. "The Course of Comecon" introduces a new element, that of divergence of interests in the bloc. This factor has become one of the dominant themes in Eastern Europe today.

The concluding part of this section contains two pieces on the reaction in Eastern Europe to the fall of Khrushchev. These selections also touch on factors which may prevent the restoration of Communist unity in the bloc.

1. The Years of Trouble: 1945-1956

THE COMMUNIST TAKE-OVER [1]

How did the Communists take power in Eastern Europe?

There is certainly no mystery about the long-standing ambitions of Russia—both Czarist and Soviet—in the area. This was made plain when, in September 1939, the U.S.S.R. forcibly reclaimed territories in eastern Poland which it had lost during the Russo-Polish war of 1920, and again in June 1940, when a peremptory demand was made upon Rumania to cede Bessarabia, Bukovina and the Hertza district to the Soviets. Still, it is doubtful that Joseph Stalin had formulated a long-term plan of conquest even when the tide of war turned after the battle of Stalingrad in November 1942.

As the war in Europe rolled on to its conclusion, it became readily apparent that the Red army was gaining possession of the entire area. Six weeks before the Allied landings in Normandy, it stood in Eastern Poland, Rumania and on the Czechoslovak border. Only fifteen days after the liberation of Paris on August 25, 1944, Soviet forces occupied all of Bulgaria. In September 1944 they entered Yugoslavia, and in October, Czechoslovakia. . . .

[1] From *Eastern Europe—A New Orbit?* pamphlet by Robert Bass, specialist on Communist affairs. (Headline Series. no 168) Foreign Policy Association. 345 E. 46th St. New York, N.Y. 10017. D. 20, '64. p 7-13. Copyright, 1964 by Foreign Policy Association, Inc. Reprinted by permission.

If it is obvious that the presence of Soviet troops and the widespread use of police terror were major ingredients in the ultimate Communist seizure of state power, it is well to remember also that these factors do not completely explain Moscow's success.

There was, first of all, the shield of Soviet diplomacy which blocked the implementation of the Yalta and Potsdam agreements [which contained, among other things, provisions for the establishment of representative governments in Eastern Europe] and paralyzed the work of Allied Control commissions in the former enemy countries, an armor which would have been difficult to pierce short of the use of military force against the U.S.S.R. And, as the Russians also knew, the use of force was hardly possible in the atmosphere surrounding the creation of the United Nations and in circumstances where demobilization and economic reconstruction were the prime public concerns in the United States and Western Europe respectively.

There was also the use of and, indeed, Soviet insistence on the formation of coalition governments in each of the Eastern European states. The concept was neither unknown nor inherently objectionable since it was in precisely this fashion that many Western countries were governed before and during the war. Nor was it unreasonable to claim some Communist representation in governments of national unity because Communists, at least since 1941, had played a prominent role in anti-German resistance and could, in a country like Czechoslovakia, really claim a mass following among workers and intellectuals. It was not necessarily an undemocratic demand either, and this fact made it difficult for Western diplomacy and the domestic foes of Communist ambitions to withhold acceptance. What was not realized immediately was that this was a tactic which had already been used extensively by the Communists for the purposes of infiltrating and capturing control of mass organizations during the 1920's and 1930's. The key difference was that the technique when first employed was applied to trade unions, youth organizations, literary circles and women's clubs; now it was used to take control of the governmental machinery.

The purposeful and ruthless manner in which the Soviets and their local supporters moved to decimate their opponents was foreshadowed by Russian refusal to assist the Polish Home Army during the Warsaw uprising against the German occupation forces in August and September 1944. [See "The Warsaw Rising" in Section I, above.] This callous and calculated act allowed most of the indigenous non-Communist resistance to be destroyed by the Germans. Moscow had already established the Polish Committee of National Liberation (the Lublin Committee) as a provisional government composed of Communist and Russian-oriented Poles and saw to it that the committee's hold was not materially weakened even by the inclusion, after the Yalta and Potsdam conferences, of several members of the former government-in-exile from London.

Destroying the Opposition

In Bulgaria, immediately after the Soviet military occupation, a Fatherland Front coalition was instituted by a coup d'état on September 9, 1944, while in Albania a National Liberation Front under Communist Premier Enver Hoxha assumed power in November 1944. At the beginning of 1945, Communists were able to capture control of most local administrative bodies in Rumania and to initiate large-scale purges of their political opponents on real or imaginary charges of Nazi collaboration and pro-Fascist leanings or associations. This was followed in March 1945 by a Soviet ultimatum demanding the creation of a coalition government in which Communists would hold the most important portfolios.

In Hungary, where the native Communist movement was particularly weak, Soviet pressures nevertheless brought about the creation of so-called Peoples' Courts in February 1945. Their work in purging the country of Fascists and "reactionaries" was conveniently assisted by the Russian occupation forces, which proceeded to arrest and to deport an estimated 150,000 persons. When national elections were held in November, the popular Smallholders party (peasant) obtained 57 per cent of the vote despite some irregularities at the polls, as against 17 per cent for the Communists. Nevertheless, the Soviet Union was able to insist that a national coalition government remain in existence and that a Communist occupy the Interior Ministry and with it receive control over the police and security organs.

Communist prospects for success without direct intervention were brighter in Czechoslovakia. Here, a large industrial labor force, strongly Slavophile, gave the party 38 per cent of the popular vote in free elections in May 1946, thereby making it the largest party and legally entitled to preponderant influence in the government of President Eduard Benes. But the same could not be said of the elections which took place in Bulgaria and Rumania in the fall of 1946 and in Poland in January 1947. Massive voter intimidation, police action against rival parties and candidates, and active intervention by Soviet military contingents were all used to secure the desired Communist majorities in each case. Western protests over the violation of the Yalta agreement were rejected as unwarranted "interference" in the internal affairs of these states.

This general trend of events continued and actually gathered momentum during 1947 until the entire concept of the multiparty system had been reduced to a fiction. In hard fact, local Communists had come into effective possession of all political power throughout Eastern Europe—except for Czechoslovakia, which was not yet entirely under Communist domination. Here, both the Czech Communists and Moscow were at first encouraged by the success of the local party in open balloting. They seem, therefore, to have cherished some hope that they could institute a Communist government by parliamentary means. At the same time, however, they preferred not to take any risks, and, throughout 1946 and 1947, built positions of strength in mass organizations such as the trade unions. In November 1947 a crisis over policy arose betwen the democratic parties of the National Front and the Communists, and it ended with a coup d'état that brought the Communists into full power in February 1948. This left them in unchallenged control of the most democratic and industrially advanced country in Eastern Europe and free to impose upon it, in May 1948, a Constitution closely patterned on that of the Soviet Union.

"Salami Tactics"

What the Communists had accomplished in Eastern Europe during this period was not only a ruthless seizure of power: it was also a political maneuver of considerable skill. The region was predominantly agricultural and Catholic, and much of it was traditionally hostile to Russia. The Communists were in a clear minority everywhere and probably harbored few illusions about the amount of popular appeal which they could marshal. Hence, they set about to destroy their political opponents piecemeal, starting at the right of the political spectrum and finally ending with massive purges within their own ranks, which followed Marshal Tito's break with Stalin and the defection of Yugoslavia from the Soviet bloc in 1948. Force, intimidation and fraud were certainly used where convenient, but it is important to understand that these were by no means the only instruments employed.

As in the rest of Europe, there was a strong revulsion against Nazism and fascism, and this enabled the Communists to move vigorously against many individuals who had compromised themselves even slightly. Skillful propaganda discredited many who had stood by passively during the wartime years.

Then, too, the end of the war kindled widespread expectations of social and economic reform in Europe and throughout the world. Public opinion was therefore inclined to accept the nationalization of industry as a "progressive" step and to endorse expropriation of property, especially of large landed estates in an area such as Eastern Europe where peasant land hunger still lingered and class distinctions had remained rigid and wide.

Outwardly, moreover, the legal fiction of coalition government was preserved even when the opposition parties were reduced to completely pliant bodies. Insisting from the very first on the formation of "national front" coalitions in each of the countries to assure at least a decisive share of political power for themselves, the Communists used the "unity" slogan to excellent effect in arguing that no other political approach was really possible given the tremendous effort required by postwar national reconstruction. By constantly seizing the initiative, or at least seeming to do so through the clever use of propaganda, they could thus make it appear to the unwitting that any dissent from their own proposals was divisive and reprehensible even when, paradoxically, the opposition to their course came from the majority. The unity theme thus became a political stick with which to beat conservatives, moderates and, eventually, even the Socialists into submission by the use of what—in an unhappily felicitous phrase— the leader of Hungary's Communists, Matyas Rakosi, once described as "salami tactics."

CREATING THE "PEOPLES' DEMOCRACIES" [2]

The political system set up in five East European satellite states [only Poland, Czechoslovakia, Hungary, Rumania, and Bulgaria are considered in this article] was closely copied from that of the Soviet Union. The new regimes were known as "peoples' democracies" rather than "socialist republics," because only the seizure of power had been completed, and the tasks of "building socialism" still lay ahead. But power was exercised by the Communist parties in essentially the same way, and through essentially the same institutional framework, as in the Soviet Union. The councils of ministers, legislative assemblies, ministerial bureaucracies and courts of law were completely subordinated to the party, through the party members who held the key positions in them. The armies and police forces were in Communist hands. The press, book publication and broadcasting were used by the party as means of propaganda to indoctrinate the whole population. The schools were regarded as a political weapon, to mold the minds of children and turn them against their parents. Conflict with the Christian churches and with Islam was inevitable. Religious services were permitted, but religious influence was increasingly excluded from the schools,

[2] From *The New Imperialism*, by Hugh Seton-Watson, professor of Russian history in the School of Slavonic and East European Studies, London University. Dufour Editions. Chester Springs, Pa. '62. p 83-9. © 1961 by Hugh Seton-Watson. Reprinted by permission.

and various measures were taken to make it difficult for adult citizens to practice their religions. The leaders of the churches were accused of political activity against the regime. Some were publicly tried and condemned, others were removed from their posts and interned.

The Communists introduced centralized economic planning, based on Soviet experience. Priority was given to heavy industry, and the cost was borne by forcing both workers and peasants to work at low real wages. The trade unions were means for mobilizing industrial manpower and enforcing labor discipline. They were designed not to uphold the workers' interests against their employers, but to impose the will of the employer-state on the workers. An elaborate structure of welfare services was created, but its practical value to the workers depended on the decision of the Communist party at each particular moment. At times the party . . . handed out material concessions; at times it exhorted the workers to tighten their belts. There was no question of workers influencing the leaders of trade unions or of the party. The peasants paid their share of the cost by compulsory deliveries of farm goods at artificially low prices, and the government then sold these to the consumers at a great profit. From 1949 onwards pressure was increased to make peasants enter collective farms. The means used varied from discriminatory taxation to physical force and arrests of unwilling farmers. The most rapid progress was made in Bulgaria, the least in Rumania.

Not only were the peoples of the five countries placed under regimes which were copies of the Soviet regime; their countries were controlled and exploited by the Soviet Union. The economic ministries, the police forces, and the armies had "Soviet advisers" attached to them, who were empowered to intervene as they thought fit. Some of these men were Russians, others were Soviet citizens who had been born in the country—for instance, Bulgarians who had lived for twenty years in exile in the Soviet Union. The most striking example of all was Marshall Konstantin Rokossovski, an outstanding military leader of the Red Army in the Second World War, who had been born of Polish parents, and was in 1949 appointed Minister of War in Poland

and became a member of the Politburo of the Polish Communist party.

The Communist parties themselves were organized exactly as the CPSU [Communist Party of the Soviet Union]: their "statutes" were virtual translations of the statute of the CPSU. In the late 1940's the "cult of personality" was at its height, and each satellite party had to have its "little Stalin" (Gottwald in Czechoslovakia, Rakosi in Hungary, Bierut in Poland, Dimitrov and then Chervenkov in Bulgaria, Gheorghiu-Dej in Rumania). The parties were also obliged to carry out purges on instructions from Moscow. The quarrel between the Soviet and Yugoslav Communists in 1948, which led to the excommunication of Marshal Tito by the Cominform, was followed by a witch-hunt against "nationalist deviationism" in the satellite parties. Suitable scapegoats were found, Rajk in Hungary, Kostov in Bulgaria, Clementis in Czechoslovakia, Patrashcanu in Rumania, Gomulka in Poland. The first four were executed, but Gomulka was fortunate in being merely dismissed from his jobs and for a time arrested in comparatively mild conditions. From . . . the trials of the first four it was clear that their main sin was that they had to some extent opposed, or at least criticized, the Soviet domination of their countries. The purges of "nationalists" in 1949-1950 were followed by further purges in 1951-1952, which were especially severe in Czechoslovakia and Hungary, and whose victims included a high proportion of Jews. They were clearly connected with the anti-Semitic campaign in the Soviet Union in the last year of Stalin's life. The outstanding victim of this period was Slansky, the secretary general of the Czechoslovak Communist Party. . . .

The economic plans of the satellites in these years were designed to make each produce all the main branches of industry, and to make each separately dependent on the Soviet Union. There was a ridiculous amount of overlapping. Industries for which there were no favorable conditions had to be set up, at great cost, and maintained by importing raw materials or machinery from the Soviet Union at uneconomical prices. It would have been wiser to make each country specialize in those branches of industry for which it had an aptitude, or special advantages of raw materials or transportation. But any division of labor between the satellites was unwelcome to Stalin, as he feared that it might make for closer cooperation between satellites whose economic needs were partly complementary to each other. Whatever the economic advantages, this was politically inadmissible. . . .

The policy of forced industrialization, financed by a low standard of living for workers and peasants, was pursued in Eastern Europe for several months after Stalin's death. A new measure in the same direction was a "currency reform" introduced in Czechoslovakia in May 1953, which was designed to confiscate the savings of the skilled workers and lower the purchasing power of the whole people. Rage at this new blow, combined with a certain boldness, perhaps caused by the almost simultaneous death of Stalin and of the "little Stalin" of Czechoslovakia, Klement Gottwald, produced a short but violent explosion in the Czech industrial city of Plzen [Pilsen], where crowds of workers for some hours took over the whole city, seized public buildings and put forward demands not only for better material conditions but for political liberty. Two weeks later came the great rising of June 17, 1953, in East Berlin, which grew into a massive insurrection of the working class of the whole of Eastern Germany, and clearly expressed the demand not only for economic betterment but also for democratic government and for the unity of Germany. The insurrection was suppressed by the Soviet army. The complete failure of the East German security police to control the crowds was probably one of the immediate causes of the downfall in Moscow of the security chief of the whole Soviet empire, Lavrenti Beria [who was executed in December 1953]. This in turn led to a reduction in the powers of the Soviet security police and to recommendations from Moscow to the East European Communist leaders to use milder methods towards their subjects. There now began a "New Course" in some of the satellites.

The first and most striking changes came in Hungary. The "little Stalin," Matyas Rakosi, was obliged to give up the premiership, though he retained his office of first secretary of the Communist party. His successor as Premier, Imre Nagy, introduced a program of reforms. Collectivization of agriculture was halted, peasants were permitted to leave existing collectives, and even to dissolve collectives if a majority of members should wish this. As a result in the next year a third of the members of collectives seceded, and 10 per cent of all collectives were dissolved. The pace of industrialization was reduced, and greater priority was given to consumers' goods output. Thousands of political prisoners were released, and persons deported from their homes were allowed to return. In Czechoslovakia there was no noticeable relaxation of political terror, but the same economic concessions were granted as in Hungary, and were more effectively carried out. The result was a steadily rising standard of living for the Czech and Slovak peoples, whose material conditions at the end of the 1950's were comparable with those of Western Europe. In Rumania there were fewer economic concessions, much less efficiently carried out. In Poland there was little economic improvement, but a more critical attitude was permitted in the press and publications. Only in Bulgaria did the political terror and the economic pressure remain virtually unchanged.

In the spring of 1955 the fall in Moscow of [Premier] G. M. Malenkov, who had been associated with increased output of consumers' goods, gave Rakosi the chance to remove Nagy and place one of his own creatures in the premiership. But he was unable to return to the methods of the Stalin era. The new leader of the Soviet party, N. S. Khrushchev, was determined to rectify Stalin's error of antagonizing Yugoslavia. If he was to be reconciled with President Tito, he would have to make the satellite leaders, who had persecuted the real or alleged friends of Tito in their countries, drastically change their policies. Khrushchev insisted on the maintenance of the concessions of the "New Course" period. At the 20th Congress of the CPSU, held in February 1956, he made his famous speech in secret session, in which he denounced the crimes and follies of Stalin. Knowledge of the speech spread rapidly through the Communist parties of Eastern Europe, and in the summer of 1956 (after a version of the text had been published by the United States Government) it became known to the peoples outside the party ranks.

DE-STALINIZATION AND ITS REPERCUSSIONS [3]

By February 1956, when the 20th Congress of the CPSU [Communist Party of the Soviet Union] convened in Moscow— the first such meeting since 1952 and the first since Stalin's death—Khrushchev felt strong enough to undertake a major coup.

The fundamental import of the "secret report" he made to the Congress was to downgrade Stalin: he presented him as a paranoid megalomaniac, especially in the last eight years of his life and accused him of perpetuating a whole series of criminal acts—though Khrushchev's citation of these acts was significantly far from exhaustive. A tremor shook the whole Communist world when it heard of this violent attack, for Stalin had for thirty years been the virtual godhead of the movement.

Khrushchev had several purposes in making this attack. In the first place, he desired to give the people, and the new privileged elite class of managers, technicians, and middle stratum officials who had risen in the post-Revolutionary generation, some assurance that the sanguinary rule of terror was over. People wanted some relief from the total fear they had lived with for decades, and the destruction of the symbolism and "cult of personality" of Stalin was a dramatic means of giving assurances of relief. . . .

[He also sought] to create his own power regime, supported by his own chosen functionaries. It was, in sum, a repetition of precisely the same means by which Stalin systematically achieved one-man rule over the period from 1924 to 1928.

[3] From *The Profile of Communism: A Fact-by-Fact Primer*, edited and revised by Moshe Decter, specialist on Communist affairs. Collier Books. New York. '61. p 70-5. © 1961 by the Anti-Defamation League of B'nai B'rith. Reprinted by permission.

The Effect of De-Stalinization in the Satellites

The policy of downgrading Stalin produced uncertainty and insecurity in the minds of party officials, and raised to the surface the people's hopes, aspirations and even demands for a better life. . . .

Thus, in June and July of 1956, workers in Poznan and other Polish cities streamed out of their factories to demonstrate under the slogan of "Bread and Freedom." Polish military and police forces suppressed the demonstrations bloodily, but Polish resentments against Soviet domination and Communist exploitation were not stilled. On the contrary, four months later, in October 1956, they precipitated what is known as the "Polish October" (in symbolic recollection of the Bolshevik Revolution, which had also taken place in October).

The "Polish October"

It was, in effect, a bloodless half-revolution to meet the exigencies of the moment. . . .

The stifled resentments of Polish workers, peasants and intellectuals had become even more intense as a result of the suppression of the Poznan demonstration. By the middle of October, the atmosphere in Poland, especially in Warsaw, was heavy with the threat of violence and civil war. The frightened Polish Communist leadership saw no alternative but to recall to power, as First Secretary of the Polish Communist Party, Wladyslaw Gomulka, who in 1951 had been demoted, disgraced and imprisoned as a "Titoist," and who had a reputation among the Poles as a Communist who was slightly more independent of Moscow and more concerned for Poland's welfare than his more rigid Stalinist colleagues.

Gomulka came to power on October 20, cheered on, as the "lesser evil," by masses of people throughout the country. The same day, Khrushchev and his closest Kremlin cohorts arrived in Warsaw to the accompaniment of the movement of Soviet troops around the city. In a showdown between the two Communist leaders, Gomulka warned that the Soviet use of force to preserve the old-line Stalinist regime in Poland would lead to war and civil war. Khrushchev, evidently persuaded that this was so, and that Gomulka, a steadfast and loyal Communist for decades, was the only man who could save the situation for communism in Poland, and at the same time keep the country within the Soviet bloc, relented. Political and economic concessions were made by Moscow to Poland.

The key to this unprecedentedly triumphant defiance of Moscow by a satellite lay in Khrushchev's belief that Gomulka did not represent any sort of threat to Khrushchev's leadership in the international Communist movement and to the U.S.S.R.'s unquestioned supremacy in foreign affairs. It was not, as events in Hungary just one week later were to demonstrate, any reluctance on Moscow's part to use force in the face of what is considered an unmistakable revolt for freedom from its domination.

The success of Gomulka's regime since October 1956 has rested on one factor—the people's realization that they have no alternative. This conviction stems, in turn, from certain clear facts, such as the continued presence of large Soviet forces inside Poland as well as on the Soviet-Polish frontier, and the demonstrated inability of the Western powers to help the Polish people achieve their freedom. The regime's understanding with the Catholic Church in Poland for a minimal degree of religious liberty has also helped stabilize the situation.

For about a year after 1956, Gomulka granted various political and economic concessions to the workers, the peasantry and the intellectuals—certain foods were made more available, living conditions were slightly improved, a stop was put to farm collectivization, writers were given somewhat more freedom of expression. But toward the end of 1957, the regime began to tighten the reins again in all of these areas.

Hungarian Revolution

The process of de-Stalinization had repercussions in Hungary as well as in Poland, both on the party leadership and on the people. The people became increasingly restive and the leadership grew correspondingly insecure, uncertain and frightened. As early as mid-1953, Hungarian intellectuals and writers began with increasing boldness and explicitness to discuss the need for less party control of cultural and artistic life. They, and the people at large, were encouraged when Imre Nagy, a Communist leader who had been in disrepute for several years, became premier in 1953. His tenure in office, marked by a certain leniency in political and economic policies, coincided with the period of Soviet leadership headed by Malenkov. And soon after Malenkov's demotion and a turn to a tougher line in Moscow in 1955, Nagy too was ousted, and the arch-Stalinist Matyas Rakosi resumed his rigid terroristic rule.

This only served to exacerbate the resentments of growing numbers of Hungarians in all walks of life—chiefly the intellectuals, students and workers. As the people grew more restive, the regime grew more tyrannical. By mid-1956, the Rakosi regime, unsettled by the trauma of Soviet de-Stalinization, felt forced to make one small concession after another, beginning with the resignation of Rakosi. . . .

Inspired by the events of a few days before in Poland, groups of workers and students began to issue manifestoes for liberalization of life in their country. On October 23, may of them spontaneously moved toward key symbolic positions of Communist power in Budapest—a statue of Stalin and the headquarters of the hated, dreaded Hungarian secret police. Thousands congregated before them, pulled down the statue and tried to storm the headquarters as well as the offices of the official radio station. The secret police opened fire on the crowds, and thus began the short-lived revolution in which some 25,000 people were slaughtered.

Swift-moving events saw the recall of Nagy to power, less as a leader of a revolution than its slightly confused symbol; Moscow's decision, made on the spot by Deputy Premier Anastas Mikoyan, to quell the revolt; the subsequent Soviet agreement, in the face of continued and even growing Hungarian resistance, to withdraw from Budapest at the end of October; Nagy's declaration of Hungarian neutrality and withdrawal from the Warsaw Pact; and finally, the Soviet decision, made as early as November 1,

to intervene forcibly a second time, a decision that was imple-
mented by the return of massive Soviet military forces to Budapest
and the wholesale crushing of the revolt. In addition to the
tragic number of casualties, some 125,000 [other sources cite as
many as 200,000] Hungarians, most of them youths and many
of them Freedom Fighters, fled into Austria to escape the
certain doom that awaited them at the hands of the Soviets and
the reconstituted Hungarian secret police. Nagy himself was replaced by Janos Kadar, a pliable tool of Moscow; two weeks later,
Nagy and his closest political friends and advisers and their
families were arrested and imprisoned despite a Soviet-guaranteed
safe-conduct. In 1958, Moscow and Budapest revealed that they
had been tried in secret and executed. The Hungarian Revolution
had gone down to defeat.

Moscow's Strategy in Poland and in Hungary

Faced with defiance in Warsaw, the Kremlin speedily arrived
at a modus vivendi with Gomulka. Faced with revolt in Budapest,
the Kremlin responded with force.

The difference in response was accounted for by the essential
difference between the Polish and the Hungarian revolts. In
Gomulka, Khrushchev recognized a perfervid Communist who
was the only man who could control the situation inside Poland,
prevent the outbreak of violent revolt, and remain a loyal sup-
porter of Soviet strategic interests and foreign policy objectives.

In Nagy, and more importantly, in the revolution which swept
him to power and actually carried him far beyond his own
intentions, Khrushchev recognized an open break with Soviet
hegemony, a declaration of total independence in foreign policy
and of freedom in internal affairs. This was a situation which the
Kremlin could not tolerate on both ideological and strategic
grounds.

The clear object lesson of the Hungarian Revolution was that
the Kremlin was willing to risk Western displeasure and indig-

nation—perhaps even to risk war—for the sake of retaining its hold on the empire it has molded since 1945.

REBELLION IN HUNGARY [4]

On the day before the holding of mass demonstrations, namely October 22, a number of student meetings took place in Budapest. At the most important of these, the students adopted a list of sixteen demands which expressed their views on national policy. These demands contained most of the points put forward during the uprising itself. They included the immediate withdrawal of all Soviet troops, the reconstitution of the government under Imre Nagy, free elections, freedom of expression, the reestablishment of political parties, and sweeping changes in the conditions both of workers and peasants. It was learnt during the meeting that the Hungarian Writers' Union proposed to express its solidarity with Poland on the following day by laying a wreath at the statue of General Bem, a hero of Hungary's War of Independence of 1848-49, who was of Polish origin.

Early next morning, the students' demands had become known throughout Budapest. Witnesses speak of an atmosphere of elation and hopefulness. Radio Budapest referred to the planned demonstration, but later announced a communiqué prohibiting it from the Minister of the Interior. The ban was, however, lifted during the early afternoon, when the demonstration was already under way. Thousands of young people took part in it, including students, factory workers, soldiers in uniform and others.

Most of the crowd afterwards crossed the Danube to join demonstrators outside the Parliament Building where, by 6 P.M., between 200,000 and 300,000 people were gathered. Repeated calls for Imre Nagy eventually brought the former Premier. Mr. Nagy addressed the crowd briefly from a balcony of the Parliament Building.

[4] From *Report of the Special Committee on the Problem of Hungary.* United Nations. General Assembly Official Records: Eleventh Session, Supplement no 18. United Nations. New York. '57. Reprinted by permission. Text from New York *Times.* p 10-11. Je. 21, '57.

The First Shots

The following day, some of the students went to the Radio Building, with the intention of making another attempt to have their demands broadcast. A large crowd gathered at the Radio Building, which was guarded by the A.V.H. or state security police. Shortly after 9 P.M., tear gas bombs were thrown from the upper windows and, one or two minutes later, A.V.H. men opened fire on the crowd, killing a number of people and wounding others. In so far as any one moment can be selected as the turning point which changed a peaceable demonstration into a violent uprising, it would be this moment when the A.V.H., already intensely unpopular and universally feared by their compatriots, attacked defenseless people. The anger of the crowd was intensified when white ambulances with Red Cross license plates, drove up. Instead of first aid teams, A.V.H. police emerged, wearing doctors' white coats. A part of the infuriated crowd attacked them and, in this way, the demonstrators acquired their first weapons. Hungarian forces were rushed to the scene to reinforce the A.V.H. but, after hesitating a moment, they sided with the crowd.

The Armed Uprising

The first shots at the Radio Building marked the beginning of a hard-fought, five-day battle, in which the people of Budapest found themselves in combat with Soviet armor and with the A.V.H. The ordinary police sympathized with the insurgents, giving them weapons or fighting at their side. Certain units of the Hungarian Army fought as such on the side of the insurgents, but the Army as a whole disintegrated from the start of the uprising. Wherever they could succeed in doing so, Hungarian soldiers handed over weapons and ammunition to their fighting compatriots and, in very many cases, deserted, individually or in groups, to their ranks. There was no single instance recorded of Hungarian troops' fighting on the Soviet side against their fellow countrymen. . . .

Conclusions

Grievances

What took place in Hungary in October and November 1956, was a spontaneous national uprising, due to longstanding grievances which had caused resentment among the people. One of these grievances was the inferior status of Hungary with regard to the U.S.S.R.: the system of government was in part maintained by the weapon of terror, wielded by the A.V.H. or political police, whose influence was exercised at least until the end of 1955, through a complex network of agents and informers permeating the whole of Hungarian society. In other respects also, Soviet pressure was resented. From the stifling of free speech to the adoption of a Soviet-style uniform for the Hungarian Army, an alien influence existed in all walks of life. Hungarians felt no personal animosity toward the individual Soviet soldiers on Hungarian soil, but these armed forces were symbols of something which annoyed a proud people and fed the desire to be free.

Participants

The thesis that the uprising was fomented by reactionary circles in Hungary and that it drew its strength from such circles and from Western "imperialists" failed to survive the committee's examination. From start to finish, the uprising was led by students, workers, soldiers and intellectuals, many of whom were Communists or former Communists. The majority of political demands put forward during the revolution included a stipulation that democratic socialism should be the basis of the Hungarian political structure and that such social achievements as the land reform should be safeguarded. At no time was any proposal made for the return to power, or to the government, of any figure associated with prewar days. "Fascists" and "saboteurs," heavily armed, could not have succeeded in landing on Hungarian airfields which were under Soviet supervision, or in crossing the Austrian frontier, where a closed zone was shown by the Austrian authorities to the military attachés of France, the United Kingdom, the United States of America and the U.S.S.R.

Uprising Spontaneous

The uprising was not planned in advance. It was the universal testimony of witnesses examined by the committee that events took participants by surprise. No single explanation can determine exactly why the outbreak occurred just when it did. Communist spokesmen, including Mr. Kadar and the members of his present government, have recognized the bitter grievances of the Hungarian people before October 23. They have spoken of a "broad, popular movement" caused by the "bitterness and indignation" of the masses. Two factors would seem to have brought this resentment to a head. The first of these was the news received on October 19 of a successful move by Poland for greater independence from the U.S.S.R. This news was largely instrumental in bringing the Hungarian students together in the meetings of October 22. The second factor was the acute disappointment felt by the people when Erno Gero, First Secretary of the Central Committee of the Hungarian Working People's (Communist) party, in his speech on the evening of October 23 failed to meet any of the popular demands and adopted what was considered a truculent tone towards his hearers.

Soviet Armed Intervention

Although no evidence exists of advance planning, and although the whole course of the uprising bears the hallmark of continuous improvisation, it would appear that the Soviet authorities had taken steps as early as October 20 to make armed intervention in Hungary possible. Evidence exists of troop movements, from that date on. It would appear that plans for action had therefore been laid some time before the students met to discuss their demands. The committee is not in a position to say whether the Soviet authorities anticipated that the grievances of the Hungarian people, stimulated by events in Poland, could no longer be contained. Signs of opposition were evident before the 23rd: the Hungarian government had reason to foresee that trouble was brewing. While the evidence shows that Soviet troops from outside Hungary were used even in the first intervention, no clause of the Warsaw Treaty [a mutual assistance treaty among

Soviet bloc members] provides for intervention by armed forces
of the Soviet Union to dictate political developments within any
signatory's frontiers.

Violence by Secret Police

The demonstrations on October 23 were at first entirely
peaceful. None of the demonstrators appear to have carried arms,
and no evidence has been discovered that any of those who voiced
the political demands or joined the demonstrators had any
intention to resort to force. While disappointment at Mr. Gero's
speech may have angered the crowds, it would hardly of itself
have sufficed to turn the demonstration into an armed uprising.
That this happened was due to the action of the A.V.H. in
opening fire on the people outside the Radio Building. Within a
few hours Soviet tanks were in action against the Hungarians.
This appearance of Russian soldiers in their midst not as friendly
allies, but as enemies in combat, had the effect of still further
uniting the people.

Was Soviet Intervention Requested?

Obscurity surrounds the invitation alleged to have been issued
by the Hungarian government to the Soviet authorities to assist
in quelling the uprising by force. Mr. Nagy has denied, with
every appearance of truth, that he issued this invitation or was
even aware of it. Since Soviet tanks appeared on the streets of
Budapest at about 2 A.M. on October 24, it would have been
impossible for him to have addressed any official message to the
Soviet authorities, since he held no government post at the time
when the tanks must have received their orders. An invitation
may have been made privately by Mr. Gero, First Secretary of the
Central Committee of the Communist party, or Mr. [Andras]
Hegedus, the Prime Minister. . . .

Nagy Not Leader of Uprising

When Mr. Nagy became Prime Minister, he was not at first
able to exercise the full powers of that office. Only when the
grip of the A.V.H. was loosened by the victory of the insurgents

was he able to take an independent stand. By this time, the real power in Hungary lay with the revolutionary and workers' councils, which had sprung up spontaneously in different parts of the country and had replaced the collapsing structure of the Communist party. Mr. Nagy, though himself a Communist of long standing who had lived for many years in the U.S.S.R., invited non-Communists into his new government, and listened to the demands of various revolutionary and workers' councils. It would appear that Mr. Nagy himself, like the country at large, was somewhat taken aback by the pace of developments. However, seeing that his countrymen were united in their desire for other forms of government and the departure of Soviet troops, he threw in his lot with the insurgents. By this action, he obliterated the impression which he had created while still under the domination of the A.V.H., and he became a symbolic figure in the uprising, although he had not instigated it, and was never its actual leader.

Temporary Successes of Uprising

The few days of freedom enjoyed by the Hungarian people provided abundant evidence of the popular nature of the uprising. A free press and radio came to life all over Hungary, and the disbanding of the A.V.H. was the signal for general rejoicing, which revealed the degree of unity achieved by the people, once the burden of fear had been lifted from them.

There were a number of lynchings and beatings by the crowds. These were, in almost all cases, confined to members of the A.V.H. or those who were believed to have cooperated with them.

Steps were taken by the workers' councils during this period to give the workers real control of nationalized industrial undertakings and to abolish unpopular institutions, such as the production norms. These were widely resented as being unfair to workers and also a reflection of popularly suspected secret trade agreements with the U.S.S.R., which were said to make heavy demands on the Hungarian economy for the benefit of the Soviet Union. During the days of freedom, while negotiations continued with the Soviet authorities for the withdrawal of Russian troops, attempts were made to clear up the streets of Budapest, and life was beginning to return to normal. The insurgents had agreed to amalgamate, while maintaining their identity, in a National Guard, which would have been responsible, with the Army and police, for maintaining order.

Violation of Human Rights

In contrast to the demands for the reestablishment of political rights put forward during the uprising is the fact that basic human rights of the Hungarian people were violated by the Hungarian governments prior to October 23, especially up to the autumn of 1955, and that such violations have been resumed since November 4 [1956]. The committee is convinced that the numerous accounts of inhuman treatment and torture by the A.V.H. are to be accepted as true. On the evidence, it is also convinced that numbers of Hungarians, including some women, were deported to the Soviet Union and that some may not have been returned to their homes. These deportations were designed to break the back of the revolution. Action taken by the Hungarian people in their spontaneous uprising succeeded in ridding them for a few days of the apparatus of police terror. This democratic achievement of a united people was indeed threatened by a form of "counterrevolution" and it was to this that it succumbed. However, the "counterrevolution" consisted in the setting up by Soviet armed forces of Mr. Kadar and his colleagues in opposition to a government which enjoyed the overwhelming support of the people of Hungary.

No Popular Support for Kadar Government

Following the second Soviet intervention on November 4, there has been no evidence of popular support for Mr. Kadar's government. Mr. Kadar has successively abandoned most of the points from the revolutionary program which he had at first promised to the Hungarian people. On the central question of the withdrawal of Soviet troops, he has moved from complete acceptance of the nation's wishes to a refusal to discuss the subject in present circumstances. Against the workers, he has proceeded step by step to destroy their power and that of the workers' councils. Capital punishment is applicable to strike activities. The processes of justice have been distorted by the institution of special police and special courts and by the ignoring of the rights of the accused. The Social Democratic party has again been forcibly liquidated. General elections have been postponed for two years. Writers and intellectuals are subjected to repressive measures. The Hungarian workers have shown no sign of support for Mr. Kadar's government or for the prospect of continuous Soviet occupation. [See "Hungary: Renaissance After Revolt," in Section III, below, for an account of the dramatic change that has occurred since the date of this report.]

2. After the Storm

KHRUSHCHEV'S RECONSTRUCTION [5]

The events of late 1956 had dealt a massive blow to Soviet and Communist prestige. Polish defiance of Moscow's wishes belied the myth of monolithic unity and collaboration within the "socialist camp." In Hungary the most painful aspect of the upheaval was the fact that it had been the workers, the young people and the intellectuals who were in the vanguard of the revolt. Nothing, indeed, could have shown more clearly the complete Communist failure to win support from those segments of society in Eastern Europe on whose conversion the Communist elite had counted the most.

The developments in Poland and Hungary served to make clear how fragile was the reconciliation with Yugoslavia which Premier Khrushchev had effected in 1955. . . . Marshal Tito rejected the official Soviet interpretation of events in Hungary and took issue with the manner in which Soviet troops had been employed early in the revolt—well before it became clear that the beleaguered Hungarian government would try to sever the coun-

[5] From *Eastern Europe—A New Orbit?* pamphlet by Robert Bass, specialist on Communist affairs. (Headline Series. no 168) Foreign Policy Association. 345 E. 46th St. New York, N.Y. 10017. D. 20, '64. p 30-7. Copyright, 1964 by Foreign Policy Association, Inc. Reprinted by permission.

try's ties with the Soviet bloc altogether. Thereafter, Yugoslav relations with the Soviet and other Communist parties deteriorated rapidly. For a time in 1957, when the Marshal met with Poland's Gomulka and several other party chiefs, it appeared that solidarity was being restored. But in 1958 the Yugoslavs published a new party program which made it perfectly clear that Yugoslavia saw its own Communist institutions as different in kind from those of the other states of the Soviet orbit. Thus, the initial Soviet effort to neutralize the phenomenon of revisionism and to stem its disruptive effects in Eastern Europe turned out to be a failure.

This many-sided Communist setback made it appear doubtful that much could be salvaged from the wreckage. In Poland, a remarkable flowering of intellectual freedom gathered momentum during the first half of 1957. The parliamentary elections of January 1957, for the first time in almost a decade, offered voters some choice of candidates and the opportunity to reject government sponsored nominees. The press was full of crisp and often acerbic comment on government policy. Student and literary clubs flourished. In marked contrast, but quite as noteworthy, was the nearly total collapse of Hungary's economy and the equally obvious failure of Soviet diplomacy to make East Germany a genuine and viable state.

Reconstructing the Bloc

Clearly, urgent remedial measures were needed to preserve Soviet and Communist control in Eastern Europe; and if it was possible to institute them, this was in no small measure due to the fact that stability had been maintained in Czechoslovakia, Rumania, Bulgaria and Albania, where the parties and governments had not been faced with any serious challenge to their authority and had successfully insulated their countries from the virus of revolt.

The task of reconstruction was massive and proceeded on several levels. Its main purpose was to institute new methods of control by the U.S.S.R. over Eastern Europe in place of the overt and deeply resented Stalinist techniques of earlier years, which had relied so heavily on police activity, liquidation of political opponents and ideological dictation. The objectives were now sought with greater subtlety. The most urgent, if not the most fundamental, area where changes were needed was certainly in the economic relations between the Soviet Union and its satellites. If economic growth in the bloc was to continue at all, the more crass forms of exploitation would have to end because they had been a prime cause of political revolt and had turned both Hungary and Poland into economic liabilities. This called for more than simple palliatives. The fact that in the second half of 1956—and in 1957—the U.S.S.R. had extended approximately $1.5 billion in aid and credits, chiefly to Poland and Hungary, but also to its other smaller partners, was less a matter of generosity than of necessity. Economic talks during 1957 led to substantial changes in existing trade relations between Eastern Europe and the Soviet Union, all of which essentially favored the smaller countries. The U.S.S.R. still continued to derive many benefits from its economic ties with the bloc, and features of the revised scheme worked to the disadvantage of the weaker partners, but the concessions were meaningful enough to allow for substantial increases in Eastern European trade with the non-Communist world during the late 1950's and to alleviate some of the immediate causes of internal economic strain.

It soon became clear that the ambitious Soviet plans envisaged an elaborate network of economic ties designed to weld the peoples' democracies into something like a single, interdependent economic unit firmly bound to the U.S.S.R. The purpose was to substitute economic controls for direct forms of political surveillance. Parties and governments were to enjoy greater freedom of internal maneuver to satisfy demands such as those voiced by Poland's Gomulka; however, firm limits to their independence would still be imposed not merely by their formal commitments under the Warsaw pact but by steady progress toward the economic integration of the bloc.

Accordingly, by 1958 every East European country was induced to follow the Soviet lead in reassigning first priority to the development of heavy industry, and only Poland was able to resist a return to agricultural collectivization which, in Czechoslovakia, Hungary, Bulgaria and East Germany, was pushed with even more energy than it had been during the Stalin years, and also with much greater success. The Soviet Union had been forced to revise and, in effect, abandon the Five-Year Plan for 1956-60 immediately after the Hungarian revolt and to announce an interim one-year plan in February 1957, which set more modest targets. By September, however, this, too, was superseded by the news that an entirely new Seven-Year Plan for 1959-65 was being drafted, and it was then that the Eastern European countries began to modify their own programs so as to coordinate them more closely with that of the Soviet Union.

Role of Comecon

These orthodox moves, moreover, were significantly reinforced when new life was breathed into the Council for Mutual Economic Assistance (Comecon). This organization had been created in 1949 as an intergovernmental agency by the U.S.S.R., Bulgaria, Czechoslovakia, Hungary, Poland and Rumania, which were soon joined by Albania and East Germany. Observers from China and other Asian Communist countries also attended the more important meetings after the mid-1950's. [Yugoslavia is now an associate member of Comecon.] The council consists of high government officials who make recommendations to their respective governments, a secretariat located in Moscow, an executive committee, formed in 1962, and a number of specialized standing commissions for the more important economic sectors. The latter have, in turn, spawned a variety of subcommissions and working groups. Large claims were made for Comecon at the time of its inception. In practice, however, it remained powerless and inactive for several years. The motive for setting it up had been largely propagandistic and calculated to offset Russia's refusal to allow Polish and Czechoslovak participation in the Marshall Plan.

With the Soviet announcement of the "general line" of economic development in 1955, Comecon was given new prominence, and there was much talk of regional coordination and the benefits to be derived from greater efficiency and eliminating duplication of effort, but this was an abortive and short-lived beginning, made meaningless by the Polish and Hungarian events. Hence, it was only in 1957 that Comecon emerged as a serious instrument for binding the satellites to each other and all of them together to the U.S.S.R. Through it, Poland received long-term loans for modernizing its crisis-ridden coal industry from Czechoslovakia and East Germany, the two customers most dependent on Polish fuel. Several intrabloc bilateral agreements stipulated coordination of production. . . .

These steps were supposed to ensure that Eastern European economic endeavors over the next several years would be geared to the Soviet Seven-Year Plan, and that there would also be longer-range projections, looking as far ahead as 1975 and beyond. Specialization would take place within major industries rather than among them. Thus, in principle, all countries would keep their steel plants, but specialization would be introduced in the secondary stages of fabrication. In agriculture, a country such as Bulgaria would stress fruit and vegetable production, while grains and potatoes were to come from further north.

Substantial progress was actually made along these lines between 1959 and 1962. Productivity throughout the bloc was reported on the increase in this period. Hungary, in particular, made a remarkable economic recovery, and living standards there rose significantly. As visible symbols of the integration process— to which Premier Khrushchev attached great importance at the 21st Congress of the Soviet party in 1959—construction began on the Friendship pipeline, which now links Russian oil fields with refineries in Hungary, Czechoslovakia, Poland and East Germany, and on a unified electric power grid. The latter connects the national power systems of all the East European states, except Albania and Yugoslavia, with the U.S.S.R. and helps eliminate local electric energy shortages.

Political Consolidation

Economic recovery and adjustment between 1957 and the early 1960's were paralleled by ideological and political consolidation within the bloc. The promise of much greater freedom and national independence was not fulfilled in Poland. Once he had consolidated his personal position, Gomulka moved vigorously against dissenting ideological revisionists, intellectuals and students. Press censorship was tightened in the autumn of 1957, limits were later placed on the functions and prerogatives of workers' councils, and friction increased again between state and church. The fact that Stalinists were gradually deprived of their former positions of power and influence could give small comfort to those who had hoped for further liberalization. They soon realized not only that there was no alternative to Gomulka's leadership but also that he remained very much an orthodox Marxist-Leninist determined to preserve the essentials of the system and especially the primacy of the party.

Meanwhile, Stalinist regimes remained in power in Czechoslovakia, Rumania and Albania, with only minor changes of leadership evident in Bulgaria. Janos Kadar's "national communism" in Hungary was heavily diluted by his total dependence on Soviet military and economic aid. Mass executions of workers and arrests of intellectuals followed the suppression of the revolt; a sense of despondency and despair descended on the population as a whole. To be sure, there was no attempt either to return to Stalinist methods or to restore to positions of authority persons who were identified with the hated Rakosi regime. . . .

Soviet Primacy Reasserted

The Soviet Union, on its part, appeared to be moving successfully to reassert its own primacy in the Communist world. The more conservative East European leadership had never challenged the "leading role" of the Soviet party; Kadar, not unnaturally, referred to the U.S.S.R. as the "head" of the socialist camp; and when Khrushchev met with Marshal Tito in the summer of 1957, there seemed to be broad agreement on the need for unity and close cooperation between all Communist countries and parties.

The fortieth anniversary of the Bolshevik revolution was celebrated in November 1957, and the main address of the commemoration was delivered by Mr. Khrushchev. He said that "socialism is not something stagnant, unchangeable, fixed for all time," and conceded that "differences in the practice of building socialism . . . may be manifested." At the same time, he indicated that there must be clear limits to these "differences."

A week later there followed a conference of the twelve ruling Communist parties. It published a declaration on November 22, 1957, which could only be interpreted at the time as a substantial Soviet victory. This document paid lip service to the principle of "complete equality" among Communist parties and acknowledged that unity among them would be sought by more elastic means than were employed under Stalin. But it also reaffirmed the principle of the single-party state and defined the narrow confines within which national peculiarities could be tolerated, while giving explicit endorsement to Soviet Russia as the "first and mightiest" Communist country.

THE SATELLITES AFTER 1956 [6]

The events in Poland and Hungary showed two very important things. The first is that the working class utterly rejected the Communist leaders and policies of 1945-1956 and demanded national independence. The regimes claimed to rule in the name of the workers, but the workers saw in them instruments of Soviet colonial rule and totalitarian tyranny. The second is that the intellectual youth was united against the regimes. This is the more remarkable when it is remembered that the students of 1956 consisted predominantly of children of workers and poor peasants who could not have got a higher education under the prewar regimes. One of the positive achievements of the regimes had

[6] From *The New Imperialism*, by Hugh Seton-Watson, professor of Russian history in the School of Slavonic and East European Studies, London University. Dufour Editions. Chester Springs, Pa. '62. p 91-5. © 1961 by Hugh Seton-Watson. Reprinted by permission.

been that they had thrown open the secondary schools and colleges to the youth of the poorer classes. These young men owed everything to the regime. The Communist leaders had hoped that they would thus create a new "toilers' intelligentsia" which would provide the brains of the totalitarian regime and the ruling cadres of the Soviet colonial system. But the young workers and peasants had not only learned facts and skills, they had learned ideas and they had learned to think. They had seen through the hypocrisies and deceits of the Communists, and they had become more aware than ever of the sufferings of their people. In this they had in fact followed the example of their predecessors of the "bourgeois intelligentsia" who had led the democratic movement against the prewar Polish and Hungarian dictatorships. In 1956 it was the Polish and Hungarian educated youth which led the revolutionary movement. This was a terrible lesson for the Communists not only in Poland and Hungary but in the Soviet Union itself.

During 1957 Poland enjoyed a great deal of liberty. At first there were even public discussions, at meetings and in print, of the fundamental principles of Marxism. "Revisionists" questioned the dogmas of Lenin and Stalin from a Marxist point of view, and others even criticized Marx. By the summer public discussion of this sort had been stopped, but private conversations were possible, without fear of police informers or repression, as late as 1960. Workers' councils were organized in the factories, but they were gradually shorn of their powers, and by 1958 had ceased to play a role of any importance. The Catholic Church was freed from almost all government interference, and religious instruction was reintroduced into the schools. But from 1959 onwards the Communist party began a counteroffensive, and by 1961 religious teaching had been ended in a majority of the schools. Nevertheless in 1961 the church was still freer than it had been in Poland since 1939, and much freer than in any other East European country. The peasants perhaps made the greatest gains from the events of October 1956. Collective farms almost ceased to exist, and farmers received much better prices for their produce. By

1960 there were signs that the government was planning some steps in the direction of collectivization, but it looked as if the methods would be mild and the pace slow. The improved conditions granted by Khrushchev to the peasants in the Soviet Union made it unlikely that brutal pressure would be exercised in Poland. Nevertheless there is no doubt that the Poles' hopes of 1956 had been mainly disappointed by 1961. This was not, however, primarily a result of Soviet intervention. Gomulka himself had always been a fanatical Communist. He had never shared the belief in political liberty of those who had swept him back to power. He believed in one-party dictatorship by Communists. He also believed in unreservedly supporting Soviet foreign policy. He did, however, object to the use of total police terror and to Soviet intervention in internal Polish administration. On these two points he still appeared to be having his way in 1961.

The other satellites after 1956 fell into three groups.

The first consisted of Czechoslovakia and Bulgaria. In both these countries the Communist parties were well organized, and enjoyed the support of substantial minorities of the population. The Czech Communists had won some popularity by a successful economic policy which had raised living standards ever since 1953. The success of the Bulgarian Communists was due to the opposite method—consistently brutal repression.

The second group consisted of Rumania, Hungary and East Germany. In all three countries the Communists were detested by the overwhelming majority of the people, even the devotion of the members of the party was doubtful. The Communists remained in power only because it was generally believed that any insurrection would be as promptly and pitilessly repressed by Soviet armed forces as the Hungarian Revolution had been.

In the third category is Albania. This extremely backward country, with a predominantly Moslem peasant population, has been ruled since 1945 by a handful of Communists led by Enver Hoxha, its "little Stalin." His success has been due partly to ruthless terror and partly to able exploitation of the national hostility to Yugoslavia. A third of the Albanians in the world live in

Yugoslavia, and the desire to include them in a single Albanian fatherland is certainly strong. The breach between Moscow and Belgrade in 1948 was a blessing to Hoxha. It enabled him to rid himself of his main rival, Kochi Dzodze, as an "agent of Tito," and to denounce any suggestions of more liberal policies as Titoism. Khrushchev's policy of conciliation distressed him. There was never a "new course" in Albania: Stalinist methods were not abandoned. It was perfectly consistent with Hoxha's past record that, when opposition to Khrushchev's "peaceful coexistence" policy was led by the Chinese Communists, he should have taken the Chinese side. The very isolation of Albania, which has no common frontier with the Soviet Union or with any satellite, though a potential source of danger to the Albanian Communist regime, was also a source of strength. Albania has needed Soviet economic and political support in the face of hostile Yugoslavia, Greece and Italy, but at the same time it is not easily vulnerable to direct Soviet pressure.

After 1956 the economic relationships of the satellite states to each other and to the Soviet Union changed. The Soviet government gave up its practice of imposing unfair prices in trade. The Polish grievance about coal prices was satisfied, and this had its effects also for the other satellites. The Soviet-Rumanian and Soviet-Hungarian "joint companies" were wound up, the Soviet "assets" being sold at a price unknown. The artificial autarchy of the industrial plans was also abandoned. Attempts were made to coordinate the economies, and each was encouraged to specialize in those branches for which it was best suited. Economic cooperation between the East European countries was no longer disapproved. It would be too much to say that the Council for Mutual Economic Assistance, the body responsible for coordination, does not put Soviet interests first. It seems, however, reasonable to conclude that it is inspired by Soviet enlightened self-interest rather than by crude greed. The coordination also extends to the allocation of tasks with regard to loans and trade with the underdeveloped countries. Czechoslovakia and East Germany have played a useful subsidiary role in the furtherance of

Soviet economic and political interests in such countries as Indonesia, Guinea and the United Arab Republic. Even Bulgaria has provided some economic aid in Syria.

In 1960 Soviet commentators increasingly used the phrase "socialist commonwealth" . . . to describe the Soviet bloc. The suggestion of equality of status is not completely devoid of truth. Khrushchev has shown much greater regard for his satellites than did Stalin. The painful process of lowering the standards of the East European peoples to the Soviet level has ended, and the standards of all have been rising together for some time. Soviet economic progress will increasingly benefit the satellites. Yet these undoubted improvements do not change the essence of the relationship. The Communist regimes were imposed on unwilling peoples by Soviet force, and they are maintained by the threat of Soviet force.

A PATCHWORK QUILT [7]

In his relations with his European satellites, Khrushchev appears to have been guided by two main principles: that in their foreign and intrabloc policy they should give him practically unconditional support and that in their domestic policy, if they practiced any deviation from the accepted standard, they should keep it to themselves and not hold it up as an example for others to follow. Their failure to abide by the first principle caused the Albanians to be excommunicated; it was the failure to abide by the second which was so long in preventing a genuine rapprochement with Yugoslavia. (In the case of China it has been her failure on both counts which has largely produced the division.) Conversely, his strict conformity with these two principles has allowed Gomulka in Poland to proceed unmolested. Despite his willingness to accept American economic aid, Gomulka has loyally supported Khrushchev on all basic foreign policy and bloc issues; in his toleration of private farming and his unwritten con-

[7] From "A Patchwork Quilt in Eastern Europe," radio broadcast, November 1963, by J. F. Brown, deputy director of research, Radio Free Europe. Reprinted from *Scaling the Wall—Talking to Eastern Europe; the Best of Radio Free Europe*, edited by George R. Urban, by permission of the Wayne State University Press. Detroit. '64. p 185-91. © Radio Free Europe 1961, 1962, 1963, 1964.

tract with the Catholic Church he has always excused himself that these were caused by specific Polish conditions.

It is this leeway granted to the satellites that has produced the complex and varied situation in Eastern Europe today.

Prior to the 22nd Soviet Party Congress [in 1961], it had been customary, and in the main correct, to see Poland as the only satellite country which in its domestic policy showed serious differences from the general pattern. In Poland police terror, or "administrative methods," had been almost entirely dispensed with. Nearly 90 per cent of the agricultural area of the country was in private hands, the truce with the Church was still being essentially maintained. In all the other countries, though both economic and political conditions were considerably better than before Stalin's death, there still remained recognizable remnants of Stalinism. In every country except Rumania, which was to complete its collectivization soon afterwards, collective or state farms had virtually replaced all private holdings. Industry of all types, as well as artisanry, was concentrated almost completely in the hands of the state. Police terror, though not in most cases conspicuous, was ever present. All alternative centers of authority and influence had been suppressed or forced into quiescence. In every case (leaving out Albania) the retreat from Stalinism had been proclaimed, but it was not a rapid one. Except for Hungary, every country seemed content to drag its heels; and indeed, there seemed to be no hurry.

But, at the 22nd Soviet Party Congress, Khrushchev began his second bout of de-Stalinization and, using Albania as his whipping boy, revealed the seriousness of his dispute with China. In terms of satellite relations, the Sino-Soviet dispute introduced a new factor by giving to the satellites a very powerful instrument if they cared to use it. Obviously the emergence of Peking as a new center of Communist authority, and the preoccupation of the Soviet Union in trying to maintain its own primacy, gave the East European regimes much more room to maneuver than before, a better chance to secure greater autonomy from the Soviet Union and even a chance to gain some influence over her.

They could achieve this either by demonstratively supporting Moscow against Peking, or by appearing to flirt with Mao so as to wring more concessions from Khrushchev. Whatever reaction the satellites chose to make, one can assume that none of them, however concerned their leaders may have felt about the unity of the world movement, were particularly dismayed about the consequences, in terms of power relations, of the Sino-Soviet dispute.

De-Stalinization, however, was another matter. Whatever may have been Khrushchev's reasons for returning to this question so dramatically [at the Party Congress] in October 1961, some of the satellite leaders had their own very good reasons for wishing he had not done so.

To Walter Ulbricht [of East Germany] and Gheorghe Gheor-ghiu-Dej [of Rumania] in particular, Khrushchev's new blasts must have sounded like the fire-bell ringing in the night. Now that Hoxha had been virtually read out of the camp, these two were the only satellite leaders left who had enjoyed an uninter-rupted reign of power since 1945. All the other leaders were post-Stalin. Not only were these two men Stalinist by education and conviction, they were also in control of weak parties. To them, any degree of "liberalization" meant the possibility of a situation which they might not be able to control. It could be 1956 all over again: Khrushchev had obviously not learned his lesson. And, finally, there was the very pressing point that criti-cism for the Stalinist sins of the past was bound to fall on them, since the sins had been committed under their direction.

For Czechoslovakia and Bulgaria the situation was not radi-cally different. In both Prague and Sofia, though the Party lead-ers, Novotny and Zhivkov, were appointed after Stalin's death, most of the top men had been closely involved in Stalinism and, in their methods of governing their countries, had hardly shown an overpowering desire to dispense with his legacy. On the other hand, in Poland and Hungary, de-Stalinization (and the Sino-Soviet dispute) presented few problems. Poland was still ahead of the Soviet Union in the matter, a fact which Gomulka made little attempt to hide. Kadar, for his part, saw in the 22nd Soviet Congress a splendid opportunity to implement a policy of "liberalization" and of cooperation between Party and people, which he considered to be the only hope for communism in Hungary.

The subsequent policy of the . . . satellites (one now excludes Albania) on domestic de-Stalinization was generally what one might have expected. Ulbricht paid deferential lip service to the notion and went through the motions of attacking the personality cult. Otherwise he did very little. In fact he had good excuses for not doing more. In August 1961, shortly before the 22nd Congress, he had put up the Berlin Wall, obviously with Khrushchev's consent. He could plead that his was genuinely a special case, that repression at home was the only course, and that otherwise the situation might deteriorate into another June 1953 [when there was anti-government rioting in East Berlin]. Gheorghiu-Dej indulged in a masterly exercise in diversion, resurrected actual or political corpses like Pauker, Luca (both purged in 1952) and Chisinevschi (purged in 1957), blamed all the crimes of the personality cult era on them, tried to pass himself off as a national, liberal leader and immediately afterwards proceeded to complete agricultural collectivization in a quick burst in the spring of 1962. His repressive regime continues, and de-Stalinization has been quietly ignored.

In Czechoslovakia and in Bulgaria some interesting variations occurred. Though Novotny and Zhivkov came to power after Stalin, they had both been educated in the Stalinist tradition, and the politburos and central committees of both their parties were packed with old Stalinists. Nor had their previous policies suggested any real "liberalization." But the immediate responses of the two regimes to the 22nd Soviet Congress were quite different. Novotny began by making rather a large dent in the hitherto impeccable image of Klement Gottwald. He admitted that personality cult crimes had taken place, blamed Gottwald for being ill and out of touch with what was going on, and removed him from his mausoleum. Novotny was at great pains to make clear that all this had happened before his own time. . . .

Subsequently, however, in the course of exorcizing the crimes of the cult, Novotny had to allow a great deal of criticism of the "past period." What began as a trickle of criticism quickly became a flood, the discontent being spearheaded by a group of Slovak intellectuals, almost all of them Communist, who demanded the full rehabilitation of victims of the cult of personality, the settling of accounts with those responsible, and a broad measure of cultural and economic freedom. Novotny was forced to drop two of his most prominent old Stalinists in an effort to contain the discontent and to divert attention from his own deep involvement in the judicial crimes of 1951 and 1952. There followed the rehabilitation, legally but not politically, of the notorious Rudolf Slansky, the former Secretary-General of the Party, who was hanged in 1952 after perhaps the most celebrated and fantastic show trial of the postwar period. Again, by moves like this, Novotny hoped to stem the tide. But the discontent of the intellectuals continued, quietly backed by mass resentment over the deteriorating economic conditions, and more concessions were gained in the face of Novotny's reluctance and displeasure. Finally, Novotny was forced to shed perhaps his biggest single item of ballast in the person of Prime Minister Viliam Siroky, a Slovak, who was detested by the whole nation for his Stalinism, and by his fellow Slovaks in particular for his close association with the centralizing policies of the Prague regime. It should be noted that it was once again the intellectuals who led the opposition and expressed the will of the nation. But in Czechoslovakia it was mainly the Slovak intellectuals who rebelled, and here many of them expressed not only their resentment against autocracy but also their impatience with what they considered to be an excessive Czech centralism. Thus after a long period of uneasy quiet the Czech-Slovak question came up again, a sure sign that "proletarian internationalism" was in itself no answer to the problem of nationalities.

In Bulgaria, on the other hand, events took a dramatic turn much more quickly. Immediately after the 22nd Soviet Congress, Valko Chervenkov, Bulgaria's "little Stalin" from 1950 to 1956, was disgraced on charges of Stalinism and crimes of the personality cult. One year later, in November 1962, at one of the most extraordinary party congresses held for years, the reigning premier, Anton Yugov, together with seven others, were dismissed from office for crimes similar to those which had earned Chervenkov his downfall. At the same time the Congress promised a new deal for both Party and people and, if speeches were to be believed, a definite break with the past had been made. But Zhivkov flattered only to deceive. Either through his own reluctance or because of strong lower level opposition, de-Stalinization soon ground to a halt. Thus, while in Czechoslovakia it gathered momentum, in Bulgaria it lost it with disappointing speed.

THE COURSE OF COMECON [8]

Of the world's many international organizations, perhaps the busiest is the Council for Mutual Economic Assistance. Its experts and functionaries, along with the various representatives of its member countries, are constantly on the move. Time and again they descend on all the large cities of the Soviet bloc to "discuss," to "exchange experiences," to "prepare draft proposals," to "coordinate" or to "organize.". . .

What have been the practical results of this buzzing activity? In terms of the organization's objectives—very little. Even the Communist press now admits that the Comecon regional specialization scheme will not become operative until the mid-seventies. One may say, in fact, that the feverish activity of the Comecon experts serves primarily as a smokescreen to hide the lack of any real progress in achieving Comecon's avowed aims.

Those aims were clearly stated in a communiqué issued after the summit meeting of leaders of the Comecon member countries in May 1958, and in many subsequent policy declarations. They amount to the application of the principles of specialization and international division of labor to a single unified market embrac-

[8] From "Comecon Today," article by Michael Gamarnikow, an economist specializing in Soviet bloc affairs. *East Europe.* 13:3-9. Mr. '64. Reprinted by permission.

ing the whole Communist bloc, or at least to that part of it which owes ideological allegiance to Khrushchev. This scheme, if carried to its logical conclusion, would eventually lead to the establishment of a unified and completely integrated bloc-wide economy, directed, planned and managed by a supranational authority. . . .

But the question of this supranational authority has sparked a bitter conflict within Comecon. . . . The conflict arises from the basic contradiction between national and community interests. The main point at issue is whether the member states should surrender a significant part of sovereign control over the development of their national economies in order to achieve greater economic efficiency for the bloc as a whole.

The problem has political aspects too. There is a contradiction between the obvious economic benefits of specialization and the grave political danger involved in the loss of economic sovereignty and in being too dependent on the U.S.S.R.—which is bound to dominate the supranational authority of Comecon. This accounts for the fact that the East European Communist leaders are obviously not quite sure whether they want to integrate their economies, at least to any significant degree.

The lesson of the Soviet-Albanian conflict has not been lost upon them. Khrushchev used the strongest possible methods of economic pressure, including a trade embargo and a virtual economic blockade, in an attempt to overthrow the Hoxha regime. The smaller countries are acutely aware of the fact that each consecutive step toward economic integration further erodes their economic independence, as well as their political autonomy, and exposes them progressively more and more to Soviet hegemony. . . .

This major conflict turns upon four basic issues: (1) how to develop an economically rational basis for specialization and economic integration; (2) how to ensure adequate development of resources on a community-wide basis and at the same time an equitable distribution of the investment burden involved in this development; (3) what sort of over-all planning system to adopt; and (4) whether or not to accept the principle of a supranational authority. These disputed issues have been superimposed on the already existing conflicts and contradictions in the Soviet-bloc integration scheme. Their combined effect has been to reduce the progress of Comecon to a snail's pace. Another summit meeting in Moscow in July 1963, which again ended in a deadlock, amounted to a rejection of Khrushchev's grand design.

The Rumanian Schism

Indeed the only significant development in 1963 was in the opposite direction from that envisaged in Khrushchev's plan. This was the conflict between Comecon and Rumania over that country's plans for economic development. The Rumanians insisted on pursuing all-around industrial development in traditional Communist fashion and in adapting their trade policies to their own design rather than to that of Comecon. Thus the Rumanian leaders challenged not only the principle that community interests should prevail over national interests, but the very concept of a division of labor based on *the present stage of economic development* of the Soviet-bloc countries.

The chief motive of the Rumanians was, perhaps, less the desire to maintain economic independence than the old-fashioned Stalinist belief that the development of a national base of heavy industry is the necessary prerequisite for building socialism. Although purely nationalistic appeals predominated in the propaganda put out by the Rumanian leaders for internal consumption, the strong Stalinist background of Gheorghiu-Dej and his closest associates suggests that autarchic economic concepts played at least an equal part in their strong and successful resistance to Khrushchev's grand design.

Whatever their actual motives, however, the immediate effect of the Rumanian opposition was to slow down and emasculate the Comecon integration scheme. Some steps taken by the Rumanians were definitely retrograde from the Comecon standpoint, since they led to a further duplication of productive capacity. New heavy industrial undertakings such as the Galati iron and steel complex manifestly contradict the basic principles of international specialization. But the main effect of the Rumanian revolt was to break the momentum in the progress of integration and in fact to introduce the element of national veto into an international system of planning. This voluntarism, which had been implicit in the practice of Comecon before 1962, has now been institutionalized by the Rumanian actions. This means that, at present, every Comecon member need accept only as much integration as it deems compatible with its national interests. . . .

The basic problem of Comecon remains the conflict of national versus common interests. It is this conflict which prevented Khrushchev's grand design from getting off the ground. The only way to resolve it and to promote real integration would be the issuance of arbitrary directives by a supranational authority armed with effective prerogatives and a right to control. But can such an authority be set up now, when the autonomy of individual Communist parties is growing? There is another basic contradiction here, namely that between the centralist economic spirit of Khrushchev's grand design and the trend toward political decentralization which is the reality of the Soviet bloc in the 1960's.

3. *Change at the Top*

A COLD REACTION [9]

The new Soviet leaders face deep problems in attempting to restore Communist unity in Eastern Europe. . . . Not one of the East European capitals in the Russian bloc reacted to the ouster of Nikita S. Khrushchev with enthusiasm.

In each case the reaction has been reserved or even somewhat hostile. In almost every case, pro forma recognition of the new Moscow leadership has been accompanied by tributes to the contributions of Mr. Khrushchev. In a number of cases, direct questions have been raised about the manner and method of the Moscow shake-up.

[9] From "East Europe Bloc Cold to Changes in Soviet Regime," by Harrison E. Salisbury, assistant managing editor, New York *Times*. New York *Times*. p 1+. O. 21, '64. © 1964 by The New York Times Company. Reprinted by permission.

The East European Communist reaction has been almost as cool as that of Western Communist parties. The reserved attitude in East Europe casts in relief the task facing Mr. Khrushchev's successors in seeking again the kind of unity the Communist world had before the death of Stalin eleven years ago. At that time East Europe was a solid Stalinist preserve, with the exception of Yugoslavia, which broke away from Moscow's control in 1948.

Stalin's successors—Premier Georgi M. Malenkov, Foreign Minister Vyacheslav M. Molotov and Security Chief Lavrenti P. Beria—were acclaimed without reservation in Eastern Europe.

When the Soviet leadership changed again, with the execution of Mr. Beria, the demotion of Mr. Malenkov and the downgrading of Mr. Molotov, the Eastern European capitals cheered the new chiefs, Mr. Khrushchev and Nikolai A. Bulganin.

Viewpoints Now Vary

The present response to a shift in Moscow was described . . . as evidence of the distance the nations in the bloc have moved toward polycentrism—a variety of viewpoints within the Communist world. The cool reaction was also said to reflect the fact that in the years since Stalin, men strongly attached to Mr. Khrushchev and to his approach have come to the fore in the bloc. When Mr. Khrushchev's associates in Moscow turned upon him, there was no corresponding turn in other Communist capitals.

Even in Eastern European capitals that have been regarded as citadels of a comparatively "hard line," such as East Berlin and Prague, there were warm expressions for Mr. Khrushchev, accompanied by sharp questions. One Prague radio broadcast . . . spoke of the high value Czechoslovakia placed upon Mr. Khrushchev's career while wishing success to the new leaders. Two leaders went on record with expressions of appreciation for Mr. Khrushchev's role—Janos Kadar of Hungary and Wladyslaw Gomulka of Poland.

Hungary, which Mr. Khrushchev visited last spring [in 1964], appeared to display the most negative attitude. Mr. Kadar is regarded as a close friend of Mr. Khrushchev and, in the last two years, Hungary's policies have closely reflected Mr. Khrushchev's "liberal" line.

Mr. Gomulka is known to have differed with Mr. Khrushchev on the wisdom of pressing the Chinese-Soviet conflict to a showdown. But he demonstrated a warm attitude toward the fallen leader. Both the Hungarians and the Poles indicated a wish for a fuller explanation.

Rumania Is Silent

Rumania has been silent. Gheorghe Gheorghiu-Dej, the Rumanian leader, was in sharp conflict with Moscow over economic policy for nearly two years. Bucharest has reported the Soviet communiqués but has made no official statement.

The Bulgarian Communist party's Central Committee . . . officially approved the change in Moscow. This was the only Eastern European party in the bloc to take such action. Todor Zhivkov, the Bulgarian leader, rose to authority under the sponsorship of Mr. Khrushchev. Of all the Eastern governments, Bulgaria's has generally been regarded as the one most closely attached to the Kremlin by economic, political and ethnic ties. . . .

The only East European nation to hail Mr. Khrushchev's downfall was Albania. The Albanians have long considered Mr. Khrushchev their personal enemy. Albania has been the ally of China in the ideological struggle, and Mr. Khrushchev's attacks on the Chinese often appeared in the guise of attacks on the Albanians. The Albanians have accused Mr. Khrushchev of attempting to overthrow the regime of Enver Hoxha and Mehmet Shehu. Mr. Khrushchev's downfall was hailed as "a heavy blow" to the "American imperialists" and the "modern revisionists who are faithfully serving their purposes."

Yugoslavia published numerous sympathetic accounts of Mr. Khrushchev's deposition and raised questions. However, President Tito has made no public statement nor has there been any public statement by the Yugoslav government or party.

IMPLICATIONS OF KHRUSHCHEV'S FALL [10]

The Communist regimes of Eastern Europe, as if trying to erase the record of their first shocked reaction to the downfall of Nikita S. Khrushchev, put on a "business-as-usual" face this week [after the ouster of Khrushchev].

Official and press comments in Eastern European capitals, when they were forthcoming at all, achieved such a blandness that a stranger to Communist affairs might be forgiven for assuming that the Soviet Union changed its top leadership with every new moon. The superficial patina of normalcy is one of the clearest marks of the profound and still immeasurable effects that Mr. Khrushchev's fall has exercised upon the belt of ancient European nations that adjoins the western frontier of the Soviet Union. If it had been a case of normal and voluntary retirement of an aging leader—as Wladyslaw Gomulka, Poland's party chief, sought to suggest belatedly this week—Eastern Europe would have been prepared with an appropriate congratulatory response. If the Communist camp were still organized as it was in Stalin's day, the response, motivated by fear and servility, would have been even more prompt and fulsome.

The actual reaction made two significant facts clear to Western observers. The iron grip with which Moscow held Eastern Europe in the Stalin era is no more. From Warsaw to Sofia Communist leaders met within hours of the bombshell to take stock of a dismaying situation. There was no circular directive from Moscow telling lesser hierarchs what to think, so reactions varied unpredictably.

Janos Kadar of Hungary, who owed his political life to Mr. Khrushchev, told his countrymen emotionally that they had no reason to be ashamed of their cheers for the fallen leader only a few days before. Prague and East Berlin, where it used to be said that one put up an umbrella when it was raining in Moscow, officially received the news "with deep emotion." Rumania, a prodigal son in the Soviet family of nations, coolly said nothing

[10] From "East Europe Asks: 'What Goes on in Moscow?' " by Arthur J. Olsen, New York *Times* correspondent. New York *Times*. p E7. N. 1, '64. © 1964 by The New York Times Company. Reprinted by permission.

at all. Only Bulgaria, keeping alive the tradition of Stalinist toadying, took every word of the new regime in Moscow as gospel. Subsequent reactions underlined the impression of disorientation and dismay in Eastern Europe. . . .

Hasty Reassurances

The successors to power, evidently taken aback by the pointed lack of applause from what used to be the Eastern European claque, made haste to reassure the subordinate allies that nothing had really changed. Leonid I. Brezhnev, the party chief, and Aleksei N. Kosygin, the Premier, hastened to the Polish border to allay Mr. Gomulka's ill-concealed alarm that Poland's particular "road to socialism" might be questioned by a possibly more orthodox Soviet regime.

Mr. Khrushchev's era was one of national rebirth for the heavily burdened countries of Eastern Europe. He dismantled the police apparatus that made their governments literally puppet regimes for a decade after World War II. He became a permissive interpreter of the Marxist-Leninist gospel, allowing deviations to meet local needs. He eased the intensity of the cold war with the West, permitting the countries east of the Elbe to remember that they were not only Communist but still European.

The lighter hand in Moscow released these countries to enter a period of change whose end is not in sight.

Rumania took the road of classic small-power nationalism. Still a tough dictatorship internally, she has for four years been playing her cards in international affairs on the basis of strict national interest. When the Rumanians demonstratively shrugged their shoulders at Mr. Khrushchev's fall, they were conveying the idea that it no longer made much difference who was boss in Moscow.

At the other extreme, Bulgaria's stolid party leadership reacted as if this were still 1953.

In between there was a first reaction of fear—fear of a roll-back to the harsh old days, fear of a disruption of now-established practices ("I'll never get another passport to travel in the West," cried a Czechoslovak actress, weeping at the news), fear in the hierarchy, particularly in East Berlin and Budapest, of matching personnel changes in the satellite parties.

In two weeks [since the ouster of Khrushchev] these fears seem to have eased. The Brezhnev-Kosygin regime is perhaps ready to accept philosophically the disordered and contentious condition of the once-tidy Soviet empire in Europe. This may be the better part of wisdom, for most European Communist leaders regard the era of servile conformity as forever past. All will make some sort of accommodation with Moscow, for one cannot finesse away the facts of Soviet troops and Soviet oil and Soviet raw materials feeding the industrial machines of dependent nations.

Yet some of the strongest ties that bound Stalin's wartime conquests into a bloc have dissolved. This was once a bloc dedicated to and subject to the dictates of a stern ideology. Moscow's doctrinal quarrel with Peking insured the victory of polycentrism—the idea that there is no one fount of Marxist wisdom and authority. To draw a historical parallel, a reformation has triumphed over the Marxists' holy see.

The unifying force of a dominant personality ruling the Communist world from Moscow is also attenuated, and perhaps exists no more.

The troubles with maverick Rumania have demonstrated that for the Soviet Union, as for the United States, being a superpower does not necessarily make it easy to whip recalcitrant small countries into line. Where once it dictated, the Soviet Union is often reduced to cajolery and concessions to nationalist-spirited governments. . . .

This inevitably will mean greater diversity within the group. National characteristics and interests are already significant in the policy decisions of individual states. Communist officials concede privately that this trend will also be accelerated by the relative decline in Moscow's stature.

The Western experts are far from agreed in forecasting the practical consequences of the new situation in Eastern Europe. Most say that it is idle to speculate until the long-term policies of the Brezhnev-Kosygin regime are defined. All insist that the days of a fairly uniform orchestration under the baton of Moscow's leadership are over. This alone is a historic change. Further change can be expected.

III. THE CHANGING ORBIT

EDITOR'S INTRODUCTION

Keeping up with developments in Eastern Europe has become a formidable task. The former convenient uniformity has gone. In its place there is divergence, and the differences appear to be growing with every passing month. The problems peculiar to each country in Eastern Europe have emerged with greater clarity. The proposed solutions are taking on distinctly individualistic colorations. Albania, which defected from the Soviet camp, and Yugoslavia, which has gone its separate way for close to two decades, add to the mosaic. While it is still possible to speak of "the bloc," it is usually safe to do so only in general terms.

The articles in this section attempt to serve two purposes: (1) to put Eastern Europe into perspective by discussing those factors which appear to apply to all or most of the countries in the region and (2) to highlight some of the most important trends and situations within each Communist regime.

The section opens with two broad surveys of the Eastern European scene. They give a general outline of what is going on in Eastern Europe, what the people are feeling, and where the region is heading. The articles that follow deal with individual countries. The piece from *The Economist* dwells on the Rumanian "rebellion" in economic affairs and discusses the reasons behind this action. The next article summarizes recent developments in the Rumania-Hungary conflict over Transylvania. A *Saturday Evening Post* article by David Holden sketches the current scene in Hungary. The next selections consider the origins and the extent of Czechoslovakia's current problems. Two articles on Poland follow—an account of the government's uneasy attitude toward intellectuals and a piece on rising unemployment. Other selections focus on East Germany, Bulgaria, Albania, and

Yugoslavia. The section concludes with a discussion of the future of Eastern Europe by several prominent scholars.

These articles leave an impression that almost every Communist regime is searching for new ways to reach the old goals, but there is also a suggestion that the search may be forcing a redefinition of some of the goals. What this might imply for United States and Western policy is explored in the last section of this book.

NEW LOOK IN EASTERN EUROPE [1]

There is little doubt that the Sino-Soviet dispute came as a greater surprise to Eastern Europe than to any other part of the world. Indeed, the extent and nature of this conflict are still not generally understood there, and this fact will most probably delay the full impact of the break. Nonetheless, the conflict is already introducing a totally new element into East European politics.

The contention between Moscow and Peking is much more than a passing quarrel; it is rather in the nature of a schism in a world-wide movement, comparable to the separation of the Orthodox and Catholic churches in the eleventh century, or to the breakdown of Western religious unity in the sixteenth. It is an expression of deep-going cultural differences between Europe and Asia as well as an outgrowth of clashing Soviet and Chinese national interests. The doctrinal disputes which remain at the focus of international attention only reflect these underlying differences, and it is unlikely that a genuine reconciliation can take place within the foreseeable future.

The schism leads in two directions. For one thing, it promotes the division of the Communist world into two camps: one with its capital in Peking and its main support among the colored peoples of the developing countries; the other with its center in Moscow and its following among the more advanced industrial countries of preponderantly white population. But the schism has

[1] From "Perspectives for Eastern Europe," by Richard V. Burks, policy director for Radio Free Europe in Munich and author of numerous articles on Soviet affairs. *Problems of Communism*. 13:73-81. Mr.-Ap. '64.

also produced a marked intensification of factional conflict within existing Communist parties and the splinter parties. The long-range consequences of these developments for the inherently unstable Communist regimes of Eastern Europe should be far-reaching.

Ideology and National Interest

It is, first of all, important to remember in this connection that in the doctrinal aspects of the Moscow-Peking conflict, it is the Soviets who are the innovators, particularly as far as the twin doctrines "peaceful coexistence" and "peaceful transition," or such concepts as the "all-people's state," are concerned. In the pursuit of their struggle to maintain the leadership of the Communist movement, the Soviets will therefore feel compelled to insist on the orthodoxy and acceptance of their "revisionist" views, and this will be an additional reason for their dependents, particularly in Eastern Europe, to adopt a similar posture. In this respect, Moscow's official position will reinforce the latent political tendencies in the area.

On the other hand, however, Soviet capacity to ensure political conformity in the bloc has been weakened by the fact that the world Communist movement no longer possesses a single center of undisputed authority. In such a situation, the individual parties find more room for maneuver, and the risks of deviation are smaller.

In fact, many Communist regimes today have a choice of patrons; Albania exercised this option by choosing Chinese patronage. Or by threatening to switch protectors, a satellite can enlarge its freedom of action, as Rumania has shown. . . . On this level, then, as well as on the higher—Moscow-Peking—level of Communist international relations, Khrushchev encountered disappointment, for he believed that upon granting autonomy to the satellite regimes after Stalin's death a harmonious bloc foreign policy would automatically emerge as a reflection of the common ideology held by the various regimes. Instead, he found that communism as a professed creed is far from being the perfect solvent of conflicts of national interest. . . .

Increased Contacts With the West

Reinforcing certain tendencies that have been discernible in satellite politics for some time, the Sino-Soviet schism has thus strengthened in Eastern Europe the forces of revisionism, while contributing to a decline in Moscow's authority. It may be expected that in the longer run this trend is likely to express itself in the following developments: (1) greater contact with and dependence upon the West; (2) the emergence of at least an embryonic public opinion; and (3) the development of mixed economies.

Increased traffic with the West may soon become apparent, especially in the sphere of trade. Within the next three to five years, satellite trade with the West is likly to rise in absolute terms and also as a proportion of the total foreign trade of the area. Almost all the members of the bloc are already planning to import sizable quantities of grain [and several have already done so]. . . . The grain shortage which has been chronic in Eastern Europe since World War II became critical this year [1964] because of crop failure in the U.S.S.R., which has limited the Soviets' supply ability and because of the poor harvest in the satellite countries themselves. Remedial measures are now being taken in the Soviet Union—mainly in the form of increased investment in the production of synthetic fertilizers—but it will be some years before this can have an effect on average per-hectare outputs, and even fertilizers will not help soils that suffer from want of moisture.

But grain shortages are only one element in the painful economic condition of Eastern Europe. There is also the difficulty of securing up-to-date machinery from bloc sources. The Rumanians have therefore been buying increasingly large quantities of equipment in the West, and they have made it known to their bloc partners that deliveries from the West arrive on schedule and are of higher quality and cheaper. The Yugoslavs, whose economy is by and large functioning better than that of any other country in Communist Eastern Europe, now receive some 75-80 per cent of their imports from the non-Communist world. Czechoslovakia, too, would like to draw on Western industrial technology; the country is plagued, among other things, by a labor shortage and outmoded productive facilities, and it could alleviate its economic crisis by importation of modern equipment from the West. The regime in Prague, just as the Bulgarian government, has therefore indicated an interest in exchanging trade missions with West Germany. . . .

However, if they are to increase their trade with the West, the regimes in Eastern Europe will have to find new sources of hard currency, for the availability of long-term credit is limited. Something along this line could be achieved by a readaptation of some of the Eastern European manufactures to Western market requirements. Another quick, though short-run, solution is tourism. The Yugoslavs have already made a major national enterprise of the tourist trade and they now issue visitors' visas at the frontier with few questions asked. Bulgaria has built a major resort at Varna, on the Black Sea, and has relaxed visa and currency requirements. Hungary has experimented with free entry for attendance at the music festival at Sopron and visitors are no longer limited to Budapest and Lake Balaton. Czechoslovakia has opened her border with Austria to three-day visitors, and a similar practice is soon to be established along her West German frontier. Entry and exit requirements along the Czechoslovak-Hungarian border have been substantially eased. . . .

An increase in trade with the West will most likely be accompanied by stepped-up cultural contacts. Even though the Communist regimes are interested mainly in scientific and technological information, East European intellectuals are hungry for contact with their Western counterparts. Recently, for example, Slovak writers have put forward the demand that they should be granted access to Western writings in order to know better the enemy they are called upon to combat. It is a good argument, if somewhat disingenuous.

One sign of the Communists' willingness to increase cultural contact with the West is the decline in the jamming of Western radio broadcasts. The Soviets have set the example here; in June 1963 they ceased jamming official Western radios such as the

VOA [Voice of America]. The following month all jamming of Western broadcasts in the Rumanian language ceased, and seven months later, in February 1964, an end was put to all jamming of Western broadcasts in Hungarian.

Jamming has always been a costly operation, costly in electricity (which is in short supply) and costly in lost prestige. Furthermore, it makes little sense to spend money on cultural exchanges and at the same time reduce contact through expensive jamming operations. It is also hard to pretend having the ultimate in the way of a social order and, at the same time, blot out broadcasts coming from the "older" centers of civilization.

One effect of the decline in jamming should be an improvement in Communist news media. They will have to reduce the amount of time or space devoted to propaganda and increase the attention given sports, human interest stories, and news. Such changes should in turn improve the political atmosphere. . . .

Signs of a growing concern for nonparty opinion are also becoming apparent. Significantly, opinion polls have been tolerated in Poland for some time now and recently they have made their appearance in Hungary too. In the latter country, a year ago, the Communist party conducted national elections as if there were . . . doubt about the outcome; party leaders took to the hustings, mass meetings were held throughout the country, and there was a strong pretense of currying public favor. Furthermore, both Hungary and Bulgaria have shown signs of reviving, in guarded fashion, the parliamentary practice of interpellation. In Poland, recently, the regime even permitted the Sejm (parliament) to write substantial modifications into a bill on the organization of the bar which it had submitted for that body's approval.

Increased cultural exchange, the decline of jamming, greater use of parliamentary institutions, and, above all, the ever more insistent demands of writers for freedom of self-expression will all contribute to the formation of an embryonic public opinion in Eastern Europe. The most promising development in this direction would be the emergence of the writers and artists as a second source of authority and ideas alongside the party. If writers and artists are allowed to debate public issues in their work—as they are already beginning to do—the party's monopoly of ideas and information will not have been broken, but it will have been seriously infringed upon. The substance of dictatorship will not have changed, of course, but its totalitarian character will have been diluted. As long as the regimes continue to seek the active cooperation of their subjects at home and a measure of respect for themselves and their policies abroad, they will have to manifest concern for nonparty opinion.

Development of Mixed Economies

Apart from a certain relaxation of ideological control, we have witnessed in Eastern Europe during the past five years increased emphasis on improving the living standards of the people. The stick of police terror has been much less in use throughout the area and the carrot of consumer goods much more in evidence. Where industry is increasingly characterized by complex machinery and complicated processes, the positive cooperation of the mass of workers is more and more required; and whenever governments feel politically dependent on a measure of public support, their commitment to a betterment of living conditions is even more important.

In Eastern Europe a major obstacle to improved living standards has been the low productivity of collectivized agriculture which has been unable to feed the increasingly urbanized population of the area. As a result, except for Rumania, the East European regimes are partially dependent on imports of bread grains. Probably a good deal could be achieved with heavier inputs of mineral fertilizer, insecticides, hybrid seeds, and machinery, but all the countries concerned are characterized by capital shortages, and the fact that throughout the bloc the favored state farms operate in the red is by no means encouraging. On the other hand, the astonishing contribution of the miniscule private plots to national income suggests that in conditions of capital scarcity the short route to improved yields lies in the area of personal incentive. This road is also indicated by the success the Poles and the Yugoslavs have had with their state-managed private agricultures.

In the development of personal incentive the Hungarians have without fanfare taken a commanding lead. The variety of "material incentives" now offered the Hungarian peasant is impressive. To take but one example, hay is now farmed throughout Hungary on a crop-sharing basis (one third goes to the farmer) and in some collectives common fields have been turned over to individual peasant families to farm on shares. (While sharecropping may represent a retrograde practice in the American South, in Eastern Europe it has the great advantage of liberating the *kolkhoznik* [collective farmer] from his status of residual claimant at harvest time which makes him bear the risks of nature.) The number and variety of officially sponsored "material incentives" is so great that the government recently got out a pamphlet cataloging and characterizing them all. In the course of 1963 most collective farms in Hungary adopted one or another system of personal incentives, combining it with the traditional *trudoden* [work day, a system of calculating the wages due to a worker in the collective]. Hungarian agriculture thus appears to be in the process of fumbling toward a system which will be collective in form but something else in fact.

While the other East European countries with collectivized agricultures have so far done little in this respect, a few concessions to the private sector have recently become known. Czechoslovakia has restored the free market for goods produced on private plots, and Bulgaria has begun to double the size of such plots. . . . It seems likely that in the next several years we shall witness in Eastern Europe a retreat from collectivization, either in the form of greatly increased material incentives or even, perhaps, in a turn to state-managed private agriculture.

The situation in East European industry is not much better than that prevailing in agriculture. Real wages throughout the area, except again for Rumania, either remained static in 1962, or declined. The Polish, Czechoslovak and Bulgarian regimes are in fact faced with economic problems of a critical nature. The situation is worse in Czechoslovakia, where the regime has had to abandon long-range planning and accept for 1963 an absolute decline in industrial production. Except for Rumania and Yugoslavia, the short-term outlook for industrial growth is poor.

One of the causes of this predicament is the gap between Communist dogma and economic reality. It is no surprise, therefore, that in the industrial sector Communist doctrine has already begun to erode. As usual, the Yugoslavs were the first to grapple with reality. Under cover of their workers' councils [groups which, within strict limits, have some control over production and wage schedules] they began experimenting with a semi-market economy approximately a decade ago. Their success has been only moderate, but they were the first Communists to put factories on a profit-and-loss basis, to reintroduce the concept of an economic rent in private housing and to accept the notion that a modicum of unemployment may be the lesser of several evils. Their reversion to a modified market economy greatly facilitated their commercial connections with the West.

More recently, the satellite regimes have begun to experiment along somewhat similar lines. As early as 1955 . . . Polish economists . . . were talking about a "new-model" economy by which they meant something approximating the Yugoslav experiment. In the last two years, however, the Poles have actually set aside fifty-two factories to work experimentally on a profit-and-loss basis. The Hungarians last November quietly decreed the introduction (as of January 1964) of an annual level of five per cent on all equipment and stocks, to be deducted from the net income of industrial enterprises; in other words, the equivalent of an interest rate. That same month, *Hospodarske noviny,* the official economic organ of the Czechoslovak party Central Committee, published proposals involving the decollectivization of the service industries and greater over-all reliance on market mechanisms. . . .

The drift of all these experiments and proposals is in the direction of mixed economies in which induustry remains nationalized but certain market forces are set in operation. Under such a system, central planning of over-all goals would continue, but not central management. Instead of receiving allocations of productive resources at a centrally determined price, enterprises would have to compete for them in the market. Instead of being rewarded for overfulfillment of a gross output target, enterprises would be rewarded for a given assortment mix of products at reduced cost. Thus state interference with price formation would become more indirect and the price structure more flexible. It is quite possible that in the next several years one or two of the satellites may refashion their economies along these lines.

Counterforces and Countertrends

In the preceding pages attention has been concentrated on the forces making for change in Eastern Europe. Little has been said, however, about the forces that run counter to the trends described. In most countries in Eastern Europe, the greatest single obstacle to the drift toward more enlightened and humane government is the party apparatus. . . .

One country where the apparatus has so far put up a stubborn and successful struggle against de-Stalinization is Bulgaria. The present Zhivkov leadership—apparently imposed on the party in November 1962 by Soviet intervention—has been unable until now to subdue successfully the Stalinist elements among the bureaucracy. Zhivkov did put into effect an amnesty for political prisoners, but a new set of rules of order aimed toward a revival of parliamentary activity proved stillborn. He seemed also unable to enforce existing legislation providing for an equitable distribution of fodder to the holders of private plots. And while he did succeed in enlarging the size of the private plots in some provinces, he evidently thought it wiser to keep this from public knowledge for many months. His effort to improve relations with the West, and notably with the United States, was offset last December [1963] by the mounting in Sophia of an anti-American spy trial and a controlled riot in front of the American Embassy.

In Hungary, to take a converse case, the regime has moved slowly but steadily towards liberalization. The stiff opposition of the provincial apparatus was offset by Kadar's skillful leadership and by the shadow of the 1956 revolutionary upheaval. Kadar's principal weapon has been the policy of rehabilitation of the nonparty expert. Many, if not most, of these experts are in fact anti-Communist, but Kadar ruled that the past should be forgotten and that nonparty experts could hold any office in the land, except party office. By assigning them to positions as factory managers, *kolkhoz* [collective farm] chairmen, and bureau chiefs, Kadar in effect began developing a second nonparty hierarchy of public officials.

The Bulgarian and Hungarian examples suggest something of the dimensions of the problem. What Lenin called the "party of the new type" is preeminently designed to seize and hold power, but evidence suggests that it cannot successfully govern an advanced industrial country. In part this is a problem of personnel, particularly in the younger regimes of Eastern Europe where the great bulk of the *apparatchiki* [government bureaucrats] are men without university training and a sizable minority has only completed elementary school. While it is true that considerable numbers of people of education and culture in these countries have joined the party in order to continue the practice of their professions, few of these have joined the apparatus. . . .

However, the poor quality of party personnel is by no means the whole story. The Soviets have had forty years in which to educate the apparatus—and great strides have been taken in this direction under Khrushchev—and yet, the party is having great difficulty in governing a modern state.

Conclusion

To sum up then, we can expect that the East European governments, with the notable exception of the GDR [German Democratic Republic], will continue their erratic evolution toward greater diversity and a less totalitarian form of despotism. As a result of the deep split in the world Communist movement, they may feel compelled to look more and more inward, and less outward; in other words, the ruling parties are likely to become more national and less universal in character, more established and less sectarian, more concerned with the accumulation of worldly goods and less with the propagation of the faith. Furthermore, declining Soviet authority in the bloc, in conjunction with Moscow's need to establish revisionism as the new Communist orthodoxy, is likely to encourage continuing differentiation through local adaptation. The extent of the already existing diversity gives us some measure of what the future may bring: there are now in Eastern Europe two countries with essentially private agriculture, one operating a qualified market economy, two that have been receiving Western economic assistance, four where the jamming of Western broadcasts is either nonexistent or substantially reduced, one that has set out on an independent course of industrialization based in good part on trade with the West, and one that has become the protégé of an Asiatic power.

The question arises once again whether the Communist party dictatorship, as we know it today in Eastern Europe, is a suitable way of governing relatively modern and increasingly industrialized societies. When Khrushchev rose to power in the Soviet Union, he supplanted Stalin's antiquated counterproductive personal despotism by reviving the party apparatus as the main organ of control and by introducing material incentives as the principal stimulus to productivity. This pattern was followed with more or less alacrity elsewhere in Eastern Europe, and yet, today, as grain shortages, planning deficiencies and falling rates of economic growth plague the bloc, Khrushchev's response appears insufficient. As a result, the search for solutions may now lead even further along the path toward a system that would be less revolutionary and totalitarian than the present one, but more rational and cognizant of the virtues of bureaucratic efficiency. More specifically, as there come to the fore in each country increasingly numerous and autonomous groups of scientists, technicians and industrial managers—not to speak of the newly articulate writers and artists who are beginning to infringe upon the party's monopoly of ideas and information—one may legitimately wonder whether the swift flow of social development has not already bypassed the party apparatus as a useful instrument of government. There are thus in Eastern Europe important social and economic forces pressing for basic political change. Whether the change comes, and whether it will be timely in coming and peaceful, will depend in large part on the means and tenacity with which the *apparatchiki* are ready to defend their system of absolute rule.

THE MARXIST TWIST [2]

The Communist blueprint for the organization of society in Eastern Europe has undergone major modifications over the years. In part, this reflects the growth of a more realistic approach to economic and political problems. In part, too, the changes are an admission that the people are simply not "buying" the doctrines the regimes have been trying to "sell." The current state of affairs in three important areas—agriculture, religion and industry—reveals the gap between what the Communists would like to have and what actually exists. The collectivized system of agriculture is having trouble and in some countries has given way to private farming. Communist atheism has not been able to kill religious faith. And, to cope with industrial difficulties, planning methods have had to be revised to permit greater decentralization and more flexible management.

Down on the Farm

In East Germany, Czechoslovakia, Hungary, Rumania and Bulgaria the process of collectivization was completed early in the 1960's. But the results have been consistently disappointing. Before the war Eastern Europe exported grain; now grain must be imported.

In the winter of 1963-64 there was bread rationing in Bulgaria. Hungary has not met its planned agricultural targets for five years. Horsemeat has been featured on East German menus. Of

[2] From article in *Great Decisions 1965*. (Fact Sheet no 5. Eastern Europe—End of the Satellite Era?) Foreign Policy Association. 345 E. 46th St. New York, N.Y. 10017. '65. p 54-6. Reprinted by permission.

the countries that have been collectivized, only Rumania has been able to harvest bumper crops in recent years.

Unfavorable weather conditions have been partly responsible for the general failure. But there is also a shortage of machinery; and what exists is often inadequately maintained. There is not enough fertilizer or soil-treating chemicals. Above all, collectivization has adversely affected peasant morale.

Before collectivization, a farmer in Eastern Europe may not have had much, but at least he had his land. Now he works long hours for little return on land that is not his. The Communists have tried to coax more effort out of the farmers by offering bonuses and other rewards. None of this has achieved the desired results. The young people are leaving the farms for the cities. And those farmers who remain are often more interested in cultivating the small private plots allowed them than in working on the collective.

In Hungary, for instance, only some 4 per cent of the arable land is held in private plots. Yet this 4 per cent manages to produce an estimated 40 per cent of the value of all agricultural products, including 90 per cent of the eggs, 75 per cent of the poultry and nearly half the meat. Much of this is offered for sale on the free market.

Opposition to collectivization is particularly strong in Yugoslavia and Poland. In both countries, only some 10 to 15 per cent of the cultivated land is organized under the collective system.

When Gomulka, as part of his liberalization program after 1956, offered Polish farmers a chance to leave the collectives, they deserted in large numbers. Today, the private farmer in Poland can cultivate up to about 125 acres. Some 30 per cent of his produce must go to the state at fixed prices. The farmer has the option of selling the rest to the government, distributing it through local cooperatives or marketing it to the public through whatever other channels exist.

Throughout the bloc, however, agriculture remains the Achilles' heel of communism in Eastern Europe. When and how this weakness can be overcome remains a big question.

Church and State

The Catholic Church has been the cause of another nagging headache for the Communist regimes. Communism wants no spiritual competitors for the loyalty of the people. It has been the aim of the Communist governments to restrict and ultimately destroy the influence of the Church. Church schools have been shut down; church lands have been expropriated; church officials, hounded, jailed and even murdered. The governments have encouraged the formation of atheistic societies and have instigated numerous demonstrations against religious observance. But the Church lives on, and millions of Eastern Europe's 120 million people cling to their faith.

The churches are open and functioning in the Roman Catholic countries of Poland, Hungary and Czechoslovakia. Poles are still said to be the most ardent Roman Catholics in the world, and all but a small percentage of the people in Poland attend church to get married and to baptize their children. Polish Cardinal Wyszynski, who was freed from jail in 1956, has waged a running battle against state interference in church affairs. His efforts have been largely successful and there is a considerable measure of religious freedom in Poland. But it is also understood that the Church and its spokesmen must remain within certain bounds to avoid a crackdown.

Though attachment to the Church may not be as widespread in Czechoslovakia and Hungary, religion is a force in the daily life of many people in these countries. At the same time, the Communists in these nations have been more successful in their antireligious campaigns than in Poland. In Czechoslovakia, for instance, some people go to church in towns other than their own to avoid being seen.

In Hungary, church-state relations have been particularly strained. During the 1956 revolution the country's spiritual leader, Cardinal Mindszenty, fled to the United States legation for asylum. He is still there.

On the other hand, the Hungarian regime has already made an important conciliatory gesture toward the Church. In 1964 the government signed an accord with the Holy See in Rome allowing the Vatican, once again, to appoint bishops for the country. Until that time, Hungarian Communists had hoped to weaken the country's ties to Rome by appointing bishops themselves—thus implying that the Hungarian state, not the Vatican, controlled the Church. Now that an accord has been signed, church-state relations in Hungary are expected to improve.

Islam and Eastern Orthodoxy (which roughly, is similar to Catholicism, but without a pope) are the major religions in the other Communist countries of Eastern Europe. Neither faith has fared well. Not being able to draw on a foreign center of spiritual support, as the Roman Catholics can, Islam and Orthodoxy have bent more readily to Communist pressures. Churches are said to be less well attended than in the Catholic countries. Church leaders in Rumania and Bulgaria appear more amenable to government control than prominent Catholic figures in other nations.

From the Communist point of view, the twenty-year campaign against the Church has had mixed results. The antireligious drive has not eliminated the influence of the Church and, in Poland, may even have drawn millions closer to religion. Often the elderly and the middle-aged make up the bulk of worshipers at a service. In the long run, this may prove an ill omen for the Church.

How to Succeed in Business

Just as the Communist governments have had to make concessions in agriculture and religion, so they have had to revise their approach to important aspects of industrial management.

Communist officials have frequently complained of excessive centralization, inflexibility at the factory level, ignorance of market conditions and disregard of consumer demands with respect to color and style. Faced also by mounting problems of waste, overbureaucratization and sheer inefficiency, the regimes have been revising and suggesting changes in many organizational techniques.

Throughout the Communist bloc, factory directors have been told to work out profit and loss statements. Prior to this, a factory's performance was often judged in terms of whether it fulfilled its quota in the over-all economic plan for the country. Often a factory manager would be so desperate to produce the required number of units that he paid no attention to quality or the cost of materials. Customers, who were becoming more selective as the range of available goods grew, sometimes refused to purchase shoddy merchandise. Many products had to be returned to the factories.

Now it has been suggested that certain factories be run with a view toward making a profit and that plant managers pay more attention to market conditions and to efficiency in the factory. To do so, they will need more autonomy, more freedom to set production schedules and to regulate the size of their labor force. Even Bulgaria, which has shown little flexibility in other respects, has been caught up with economic experimentation and is considering revising its cost accounting systems.

Workers' councils, prominent in Yugoslavia for some years, have also been given a greater voice in some of the Soviet bloc countries. These councils act as advisory groups on production plans, and they have an interest in the plant profits—part of which may be returned to the worker as a bonus.

How should the modifications in the Communist blueprint be interpreted? Are they merely temporary measures, to be abandoned when the regimes believe the time is right for a more direct push toward traditional Communist goals? Or do the changes suggest the emergence of a new type of communism with which the West could live in tolerable peaceful coexistence? If so, then what Western policies would be most appropriate now and in the years ahead?

RUMANIAN RECIPE [3]

Proud though they are of the position they have reached, the Rumanian Communists do not apparently lay claim to any special Rumanian road to socialism. Perhaps their way has been too

[3] From article in *The Economist.* 212:1119-20+. S. 19, '64. Reprinted by permission.

pragmatic, too purely nationalist. Over the past few years it has at any rate had a distinctive look. A real spurt has been given to the country's economy; but any pressure for a more liberal regime, for greater freedom in speech and thought and wider contacts with the outside world, has been, not altogether suppressed, but firmly controlled. And in their relations with Moscow the Rumanian Communists have asserted an independence unprecedented in Eastern Europe since Marshal Tito defied Stalin; but unlike Tito in 1948 they have not had to pay the penalty of expulsion from the camp. . . .

From Russia with Tact

It has of course been lucky for the Rumanians that they felt compelled to assert their independence from Moscow at a time when the winds of change were in any case blowing softly through the Communist world and when Russia's preoccupation with China modified both its willingness and its ability to deal toughly with lesser malcontents. As far as the Rumanians are concerned, their dispute with Moscow and the Council for Mutual Economic Assistance (Comecon) has been settled—in their favor —and that is that. Ever since the summer of last year [1963] the Russians have seemed to accept tacitly the defeat of Comecon's plans to integrate the economies of member countries through a supranational planning board along lines that, as far as Rumania was concerned, would have prevented it from pursuing all-round economic development and relegated it primarily to the role of supplier of raw materials to the economically more advanced members. Last April the Rumanians issued a special party document which declared that "the planned management of the national economy is one of the fundamental, essential and inalienable attributes of the sovereignty of the socalist state"; and that in order to exercise these attributes, the state must hold in its own hands "all the levers" with which economic and social life is managed.

Upon this document, which provoked no public counterblast from Moscow, the Rumanians now firmly take their stand. But having made their point, they give the impression of being anxious not to press matters further than they must. They emphasize that they are still members of the socialist camp and have no intention of leaving it—why should they, if they can enjoy membership on their own terms? They take part in almost all the routine coordinating activities of Comecon. On all the big international issues concerning relations with the West upon which the Russians and the Chinese disagree, the Rumanians support the Russians. But there is a snag here; like a number of other Communist parties that support the Russians on general grounds, they do not approve of Moscow's tactics. . . .

Steel on the Danube

Meanwhile, the Rumanians cannot disguise their satisfaction with the way things have gone so far. The symbol of their satisfaction and self-confidence is the big new steel plant now under construction at Galati on the Danube. Preparation of the site was begun in 1961 on an immense flat plain just outside the town, conveniently near to an inlet of the Danube where a special port will eventually be built. Production is due to start in two years' time; the target is two million tons of steel a year by 1970 and four million tons is aimed at by a date not yet specified.

The chief building so far completed is a large rather elegant-looking shed, painted bright blue and yellow inside, which is eventually designed for maintenance activities, but is at present used for construction work. The building of the first of the rolling mills is well advanced, and later this autumn [1964] the installation of French and British equipment is due to begin. This joint Anglo-French undertaking will bring about 160 technicians from both countries to work in Galati for about two years. Two more rolling mills are planned, to be provided, according to present plans, by the Russians. There will also be a blast furnace, which the Rumanians themselves are building, and a steel plant, for which they are still shopping around in Western Europe.

The Rumanian Communists' determination to have a steel combine of their own comparable to Nowa Huta in Poland or

Dunaujvaros in Hungary, even though iron ore is not one of the raw materials with which (as far as is known) the country is plentifully endowed, has until recently been one of the main bones of contention with the Russians. . . .

The Galati steel combine is also a symbol of the Rumanians' determination to develop their country's economy. Perhaps the kinds of traffic to be found on Rumanian main roads provide another symbol. The three main types seem to be the forward-looking scooters, the backward-looking horse-drawn carts, and, above all, the lorries whose busy activity serves the needs of the expanding economy. (Private cars are still fairly infrequent outside the main towns, although imports last year were nearly three times higher than in 1959 and one is told that the latest status symbol is one of the bigger Fiat models.)

All the lorries, apart from the very big ones, come from a factory in Brasov which is proposing to produce 19,000 three-ton and five-ton lorries this year, and 70,000 by 1970. The factory used to turn out a Russian lorry. Two years ago it switched to models of its own design which are said to be more economical to produce and to run and—it is added, with something of a twinkle—much more modern in appearance. In Rumania the great thing is to go one better than anyone else and to go one better than the Russians is best of all.

In the current plan (1960-65) the annual rate of growth of industrial production is set at 13 per cent; so far it has averaged 15 per cent. The emphasis is on heavy industry, but the consumer is not neglected. Although a great deal may remain to be done, the serried rows of new blocks of flats in provincial towns as well as in Bucharest bear witness to the housing drive of the past few years. And the well presented industrial exhibition that is now [autumn 1964] being held in Bucharest demonstrates the variety of goods being produced by Rumanian industry, from flimsy nylon underwear to the latest ponderous oil drilling equipment.

The exhibition may be a special effort but it is not purely window dressing. In small country towns, as well as in large centers, the shops seem to be well stocked with clothes and consumer goods of all kinds. A comparison of prices with average wages suggests (even when allowance is made for the very low rents) that some of the larger articles of clothing, such as suits and overcoats, must be pretty expensive. . . .

How They Do It

What has made it possible for the Rumanians to get such an undoubted impetus behind their economic development, especially at a time when the economies of most of their Communist neighbors are running into rather heavy weather? The first reason almost invariably given is the country's rich resources of raw materials, particularly in minerals, agriculture and timber, which have been inadequately exploited in the past; particular emphasis is placed on the chemical industry, whose annual rate of development between 1950 and 1963 averaged 22 per cent.

As far as agriculture is concerned, although the Rumanians can congratulate themselves on being the only socialist country to be self-supporting in cereals, it remains to be seen whether they are yet exploiting their rich agricultural potentialities in the best and most efficient way. Collectivization was hastily completed two years ago, and many farms still seem to be having teething troubles. Leaving on one side any social and political difficulties, more mechanization, more fertilizers, and more experts are needed before the advantages of collectivization can be convincingly demonstrated. Investment in agriculture is now much higher than it was ten years ago; the amount invested in every 100 hectares has increased from 20,000 lei [about $1,650] in 1951-53 to 51,000 lei [about $4,250] in 1961-63. All the same, with a cereals production last year (admittedly not a very good one) of 10.3 million tons, it will not be very easy to achieve the target of 14-16 million tons set in 1965. . . .

Not for Discussion

As for the alleged efficiency of its planning methods, this is perhaps the most intriguing and the least clear aspect of Rumania's development. The visiting correspondent is struck by the absence—on the surface, at any rate—of any of the frank and rather agonized cerebration of the Hungarians or the Czechs on the possibility of introducing quite far-reaching modifications of the system (perhaps with the aid of some leaves from the capitalist book) in order to make it run better. Any attempt to probe beneath the surface is met by a defensive barrage of (highly satisfactory) facts and figures. It may be that the Rumanian Communists are still too buttoned up, too entangled in their Stalinist heritage, to speak freely and frankly to outsiders. It may be that their success story is all—or nearly all—that it is made out to be. Or it may be that Rumania's economic development is not yet sufficiently far advanced to have run into the difficulties that are now plaguing some of the more advanced Communist countries, and that common sense, flexibility and a pragmatic approach on the part of the planners have sufficed to keep the wheels oiled.

Evidence of all these qualities can be found, especially in the consumer goods industries where the rigidities of tight central planning have been considerably relaxed. Although the total production of varied consumer goods is still planned centrally, elaborate researches into consumer demand and consumer preferences are carried out. It may seem a pretty cumbrous mechanism, but at any rate it is supposed to serve the interests of the consumer and not just carry out the dictates of the planner.

Similarly the decision two years ago to disband the ministry of agriculture, and set up a much smaller higher council of agriculture seems to have been dictated by a common-sense realization that there was a strict limit to the amount of central planning of agriculture that could be done without knowledge of local conditions, and that agricultural experts were much more useful down on the farm than sitting at their desks in Bucharest. All but a few of the 2,500 technical experts formerly in the ministry are now working on collective or state farms, with their exile made palatable by various material and fiscal inducements.

There are also, on the human level, a number of factors which to a greater or lesser extent must have helped in recent years to put a greater impetus behind the country's economic development. While for the ordinary workers there are various financial incentives (and more in the shops to spend the money on), for the increasing army of engineers and technicians there is the additional satisfaction of being provided with the most up-to-date equipment on which to exercise their skill. Whether inside or outside the party, one suspects that these men will become an increasingly influential force in the country. Moreover, party membership and class background are becoming less important; what is coming to matter increasingly is ability and finding the best man for the job. In one factory visited by your correspondent only one of the four chief engineers was now a party member, whereas not so long ago they all were. At the universities the former heavy discrimination in favor of students of working class origin was quietly done away with two years ago.

Clearly, for most Rumanians life is better and more hopeful than it was only a few years ago. One may presume that the regime is on better terms than it used to be with the people it rules both because of its material successes and because of the prestige gained through standing up to the Russians. The sadly delayed release of political prisoners last spring was no doubt one sign of the regime's more relaxed and confident attitude, although there may have been other motives as well. In a slow, cautious and tightly controlled way, President Gheorghiu-Dej is feeling his way towards a more liberal regime. He may argue that from everyone's point of view, and not just the party's, it is better for the country's eyes to be kept firmly fixed on the goal of greater economic prosperity and not be distracted by any Hungarian or Polish type experiments. After all, he may say, the mixture of nationalism and economic expansion plus a small dash of liberalization seems to be agreeing well enough with the Rumanian people.

It is difficult for the brief visitor to Rumania to argue about what does or does not agree with the Rumanian people; the opportunities for frank and free nonofficial contacts are so much less than in some other countries of Eastern Europe. But one cannot help wondering why, in spite of all its self-confidence, the government still seems so reluctant to allow Rumanians more opportunities to widen their horizons and test their own standards and experiences against those of other countries. The publication of large quantities of translations of Shakespeare, Chaucer, Dickens and George Eliot is not a satisfactory answer, especially so long as so little modern literature is published. And the argument that the government cannot afford the foreign currency for travel abroad is not very satisfactory either—unless one assumes that a quite improbably large number of Rumanians would want to rush abroad if they got the chance.

All this is not to deny that there is a considerably more relaxed attitude with regard to contacts with Westerners and Western culture than a few years ago. It is merely to argue that the favorable impressions—inevitably in the circumstances rather hasty and superficial—left by a short visit to Rumania would be strongly reinforced if progress towards a freer regime did not lag so cautiously behind the economic achievements.

TROUBLE OVER TRANSYLVANIA [4]

Rumania, in its own inimitable fashion, offers an instructive sampling of the tensions and contradictions that are tearing the Communist world apart. In this country, a general restiveness and political opportunism have gone so far that criticism of Moscow's leadership has taken more or less official forms.

Shortly after the return of a Rumanian delegation that had been dispatched to Peking early . . . [in 1964] in an attempt to mediate the Sino-Soviet dispute, the Rumanian Workers' Party published a fifty-page declaration on its position with regard to the international Communist movement. The tract was explicitly directed against the Khrushchevian doctrine of apportioning economic activities to individual nations within the Communist bloc. As a declaration of economic independence, the document was

[4] From article by George Bailey, correspondent for *The Reporter*. *The Reporter*. 31: 25-30. N. 19, '64. Copyright 1964 by The Reporter Magazine Company. Reprinted by permission.

anticlimactic. In the first five years of its drive to achieve "rapid and comprehensive industrialization," Rumania had already doubled its volume of trade with non-Communist countries while reducing its trade volume with Communist countries by one quarter. Within the same period Rumania had spent roughly half a billion dollars for industrial plant, equipment, and employment of technicians from the West, and more than a billion dollars have been earmarked for purchases in the West during the next five-year period. Moreover, at a time when all other satellite countries were sharply reducing their trade with China, Rumania actually increased its China trade appreciably. In effect, Rumania had already become another Yugoslavia, a comparison that has been heightened by Yugoslavia's recent accession to Comecon as an associate member, while Rumania has been loosening its ties with that economic organization of the Eastern bloc.

But the declaration last April was much more than a formulated insistence on "economic self-determination." It was a manifesto proclaiming "the basic principles of the new type of relations between socialist countries" and ruling out interference of any kind from any quarter in the political and cultural as well as the economic affairs of a "socialist and therefore truly sovereign country." The manifesto turned the Soviet prescription for collective action inside out, since it declared foreign policy an inviolable part of individual state sovereignty.

Above all, coming as it did in the form of a report on the mission to Peking and a subsequent stopover in the Crimea, it took on the color of an official ruling on the Sino-Soviet dispute. In this sense, while professing incidental preference for some of the Russian arguments, the Rumanian leadership found for China. . . .

In fact, the Rumanian Communists have outwitted and outmaneuvered the Soviet Union at virtually every turn in a long course of events extending at least as far back as the 1952 ouster of the Moscow loyalist Ana Pauker and her clique. Then, or not long afterward, they reverted to their native tradition of circumspect double-dealing and discreet intrigue. Among the switches and shifts of the ideological shell game that ensued, there was none more successful than the Rumanian substitution of de-Russification for de-Stalinization. To the delight of the Russophobe populace, by 1963 the Rumanian authorities had liquidated the Gorki Institute of Russian Studies, the Russian bookstore, the Rumanian edition of the Soviet magazine *New Times,* and the obligatory study of the Russian language in all schools and universities. Since then virtually all Russian street and place names have disappeared.

But de-Russification is merely one of the many negative aspects of Rumanization. Acting ostensibly as the honest and impeccably Communist broker between the Soviet Union and China, the Rumanians have actually cleared the way for their own traditional brand of supernationalism. . . . The Rumanian talent for divisiveness has nowhere been more evident than in the handling of the oldest Balkan problem of them all: Transylvania.

It has long been axiomatic that great powers adjust Balkan borders to suit their own purposes. This is particularly true of Transylvania, which has been passed back and forth almost as often as a bottle at a Balkan party. In the Treaty of Trianon, 1920, the Western Allies dismantled the Austro-Hungarian Empire, stripping Hungary of two thirds of its territory and almost one third of its population and ceding the greater part of both to Rumania. With the Vienna Award of 1940, Hitler gave the northern half of Transylvania, including its capital city of Cluj, back to Hungary and so stimulated a competition between Hungary and Rumania for Nazi favor in the field against the Russians, the Hungarian troops fighting for the addition of the southern half of Transylvania, the Rumanians fighting for the return of the northern half. Similarly, the Soviets at the close of the Second World War restored the Trianon border between Hungary and Rumania, calculating that this would tend to offset the Soviet Union's annexation of Bessarabia and the Bukovina from Rumania on the east and provide a popular national issue favoring the Communist-dominated government in Rumania; furthermore, the consequent failure of the not-yet Communist Hungary to obtain any sort of satisfaction on Transylvania might weaken the leading Smallholders' party, which was the main obstacle in the way of a Communist take-over in Hungary. Like Hitler, the Soviets sought to use the Transylvanian issue as a means of keeping both Hungary and Rumania under control.

Naturally, there are a great many people who consider themselves Hungarians now living in Rumanian territory. More than half a million of them inhabit the strip of territory some thirty miles wide along the Hungarian-Rumanian border. This area, properly speaking, is not and never was part of Transylvania. It is made up of four counties of the old Kingdom of Hungary and is geographically an extension of the central Hungarian plain. The other main concentration of Hungarians in Rumania is the solid block of Szeklers, some 700,000 strong, who have inhabited most of eastern Transylvania since the tenth century. The Szekler area lies almost exactly in the center of Rumania, more than one hundred miles to the east of the Hungarian border. King Carol [of Rumania] had agreed to cede the border area—the so-called "Partium"—to Hungary even before the Vienna Award was forced upon him, and the Hungarians had great hopes that the Soviets would undertake some doctoring of the border, especially after Hungary became Communist.

Instead the Soviets chose to provide an object lesson in Marxism-Leninism by applying the principle of "genuine proletarian internationalism for all Communists" to the 1.7 million Hungarians in Rumania, who constitute the largest ethnic minority in Eastern Europe. Thus, Article 82 of the Rumanian constitution of 1952 provides that "Every individual national group may freely make use of its own language, and may freely visit at every level those institutions of general education in which instruction is given in its mother tongue . . . ," and Articles 19, 20, and 21 attempted to solve the millennial problem of the Szeklers through the creation of the Autonomous Hungarian Region. Modeled on the autonomous regions within the individual Soviet Republics, it was clearly meant to serve as a showpiece of "genuine proletarian internationalism." Communist functionaries from Moscow, Bucharest, and Budapest converged on the region. Stakhanovites [workers who excel in production] from all three countries were sent to instruct and inspire the workers, youth brigades were organized, factories and roads were built, farmers were persuaded or forced to join collectives. But then came the Hungarian revolt.

In retrospect, it is apparent that the Hungarian revolt in the fall of 1956 was the turning point in the course of communism in Europe. Establishing the Hungarians as the archculprits in the eyes of the Soviets, it provided the Rumanian Communist party with a classic opportunity to demonstrate its loyalty to the Soviet Union. The Rumanian Communists were in a position to render the Soviet Union a signal service in playing host to Imre Nagy, Pal Maleter, and other leaders of the Hungarian revolt during their long incarceration and subsequent execution, relieving the Russians of the onus of deporting the rebels to the Soviet Union. They were also able to help the Soviet Union in Hungary by sending Hungarian-speaking goon squads to Budapest and the provinces to reinforce the decimated and thoroughly demoralized Hungarian Security Service.

At the same time, the Hungarian revolt thoroughly alarmed the Rumanian Communists. The reason was simple enough: the same anticommunism that exploded in Hungary immediately spread to the Hungarian minority in Rumania. As in Hungary, students, teachers, and university professors were in the forefront of the action. There were student demonstrations in Cluj, in Medias, in Timisoara, and in the administrative center of the Hungarian Autonomous Region, Tirgu Mures—in fact in every area where there were Hungarian students in any numbers. Furthermore, the revolt threatened to catch fire among the Rumanian peasantry and the country's intellectuals. Some of the more circumspect Rumanians were only waiting to see whether the West would support Hungary. When that didn't happen, the Hungarians were obviously doomed.

There followed the Soviet isolation of Hungary and the branding of the Hungarians as Fascists and chauvinists. The Rumanians were quick to take the Soviet cue, exploiting the official condemnation of the Hungarians to the hilt and applying it particularly to the Hungarian minority in Rumania. For the moment the Hungarian minority in Rumania rose in sympathy with the Hungarian revolution, Rumanians tended to see the whole thing as part of the old campaign for the annexation of territory in Transylvania to Hungary. Thus the Rumanian Communist party was not only fighting for its life, it was also fighting for what every Rumania considers Rumanian national territory.

Russians troops put down the disorder in Rumania and thousands of Hungarians were arrested, perhaps hundreds put to death. In one trial alone in Cluj, thirteen out of fifty-seven accused were executed. This year some eight thousand political prisoners were released with considerable fanfare by the Rumanian government in a general amnesty. But as far as I could ascertain in my recent travels through Transylvania, not one of the Hungarians arrested during the revolt has yet been released.

The Capital of Limbo

Two years after the revolt, the Rumanian government received the great and all-important prize for loyalty and services rendered to the Soviets—the withdrawal of the Red Army. "Genuine proletarian institutionalism" is also gone, and the Rumanian desire to keep the Hungarian minority in its place has found more and more ways of expressing itself. In 1959, the rector of the Bolyai University, Professor Lajos Takacs, expressed his regret over the "nationalist isolation" of the Hungarian minority and requested the ministry of education "to examine the advisability of having two universities in Cluj." In June, 1959, the students and professors "unanimously approved" the merger of their university with the Rumanian Babes University.

Late in 1960, the Rumanian government undertook the administrative reorganization of the entire country, ostensibly to effect a more rational economic division among the various territories. Actually, the reorganization achieved the ethnic gerrymandering of the Autonomous Hungarian Region, and the authorities have used economic measures to break up the Szekler communities and disperse the fragments throughout the country.

The closing of Hungarian cultural institutions has also continued. The six-hundred-year-old Hungarian college at Aiud was closed and its library impounded. In 1962 the last Hungarian institution of higher learning, the Institute of Medicine and Pharmacy at Tirgu Mures, was liquidated outright; the Rumanian authorities did not even bother to cloak the operation as a merger. The liquidation was officially described as "the reduction of Hungarian-language classes" at the institute.

It was in 1962 that the Rumanians launched their main administrative assault against the Autonomous Region. All key positions in administration and industry were taken over by Rumanians. Dimitru Puni, a Rumanian, was appointed chairman of the regional people's council. The Hungarian Writers' Association in Tirgu Mures was merged with a Rumanian Writers' Association imported for that purpose. In the same way, the Szekler State Theatre was enlarged by the addition of a Rumanian section. The most far-reaching measure, however, was the merging of Hungarian with Rumanian schools. By the end of 1962 there was no longer a single wholly separate Hungarian school in Rumania. Within two years the new dispensation had made a mockery of the constitution's guarantee of access to schools where instruction is given in each people's "mother tongue." Rumanian has effectively replaced Hungarian at every level as the language of official and public life. This is not only because the leaders and key functionaries of the region are all Rumanians who know no Hungarian; employees throughout the region have been put on notice that if they fail to use Rumanian in public they will be summarily dismissed.

I have seen how these regulations work. When I stepped into a shop in Tirgu Mures and addressed the salesclerk in Hungarian, he answered in Rumanian. I persisted in Hungarian. He persisted in Rumanian. Finally I asked him if he spoke Hungarian. "Whenever I can," he answered in Hungarian, "but we are under orders to speak Rumanian to customers." I asked if Tirgu Mures was not the capital of the Hungarian Region. "This is the capital of Limbo," he replied.

HUNGARY: RENAISSANCE AFTER REVOLT[5]

The train from Vienna to Budapest was packed with Hungarians going home. As it rolled out of the Ostbahnhof, past the prosperous apartment blocks of postwar Austria, the passengers fell silent, gazing through their own flickering reflections at the last of the Western world rushing by them. This was the moment for remembering.

For all of them there were pictures to recall of the trip to the West—of tearful family reunions and nights out in London or Paris. For many there must have been older memories, scars that would never be erased but could now at last be contemplated without anguish. Memories of sons and brothers, friends and neighbors who had fled the other way to freedom almost eight years ago. Men and women who had dragged themselves through the winter mud of the Danube plain, sneaked past the guards and the wire, huddled in the ditches as the bullets whipped overhead. Memories perhaps of some who never made it, shot down at the last stride—and of 200,000 compatriots who did, scrambling frightened, bitter and exhausted across the Iron Curtain, leaving a prison behind.

They have scattered now, those refugees of 1956. In the United States and Canada, in Britain and France, Australia and South America, they have joined the great ranks of the displaced, the victims of persecution and oppression who have escaped to fight again elsewhere. But the Iron Curtain remains. You can see it, in all its old symbolic menace, from a corner of the Austro-Hungarian frontier near the Danube, just forty-five minutes' drive eastward from Vienna. The watchtowers straggle up the hills from the river like spidery, immobile visitors from outer space, as if ready to pounce on any human movement. The barbed wire threads a black web between them, and from a distance you may hear the bark of kenneled guard dogs impatient for action.

This was the scene of the great flight, as the Russian army with brutal efficiency suppressed the rebellion of the late Imre

[5] From article by David Holden, a British writer on foreign affairs. *Saturday Evening Post.* 237:38+. Ap. 25, '64. Reprinted by permission.

Nagy and the workers and students of Budapest. Nothing, probably not even the Berlin Wall, has so colored our Western vision of Eastern Europe as the events of that grim October 1956. And it is still temptingly easy, as you stand at this corner of a divided world, to imagine what bitter depression must lie now beyond the wire, what disillusionment and hopelessness for ten million Hungarians who, by force or choice, stayed in the prison they must call home.

Such an exercise is two years out of date. All over Eastern Europe now a liberating nationalism is cracking the shell of Russian domination and Communist theory. Rumania rejects Soviet control of its economy; Czechoslovakia experiments with new cultural freedom; Yugoslavia, once bitterly condemned for being the first Soviet satellite to break away, has won Moscow's acceptance of its maverick role; and in Hungary the frontier is open to the West at last, and a nation is beginning to rediscover itself.

A hint of this new spirit emerged even as the train from Vienna crossed the border the other day. On either side of the tracks the watchtowers and the wire marched straight across the plowed fields to infinity. The sight brought the passengers to their feet, nudging, chattering, pointing, searching the view for something else that would distinguish home. They found it in the border station at Hegyeshalom, a few miles on, in the Red Star over the stationmaster's office and the uniformed customs men who came aboard and began emptying suitcases from end to end of the train. This was a moment of silence again. A touch of resentment and fear hung in the air as new German transistor radios were ferreted out and examined, and cartons of Western cigarettes were nervously declared. For the visitor, too, there was a tiny prickle of alarm at the thought of the cameras in the rack and the notebooks in the briefcase. But in half an hour the customs men had gone off to the dining car for a beer, and one of the passengers turned to me with a smile of reassurance. "All is good," he remarked in English. "We think now where do we go for our holiday next year. You see, is very different in Hungary now."

And indeed it is. The government of Premier Janos Kadar, whose supposed pleas for help supposedly brought in the Russian troops to suppress the rising in 1956, has at last opened the prison gates of Hungary, and he has been repaid, if not with popularity then certainly with toleration, if not with loyalty then at least with amiable indifference. Last year, for the first time in a quarter of a century, half a million Hungarians went abroad and voluntarily returned again. And although most of them only visited other Communist countries, at least forty thousand traveled to the West.

But the traffic is not only one-way. Last year fifteen thousand tourists visited Hungary from the United States alone. And by Kadar's decree it has been possible since last August for political refugees of 1956 to return as temporary visitors. The response to this offer has been understandably small and cautious so far, but refugees who do return find a country very different from the austere, tyrannical place they knew. The 1956 rising has won a posthumorous reward.

Officially the rising has remained what it was christened, the "reactionary Fascist counterrevolution." But unofficially some of its aims have been quietly adopted. The rebellion's leader, Imre Nagy, was executed in 1958 in a last effort by Kadar to suppress the demons of revolt. [The United Nations report on the revolt offers a conflicting view of Nagy's role. See "Rebellion in Hungary," in Section II, above.—Ed.] But ever since, although nobody mentions Nagy's name and few speak of the revolt if they can help it, the ghosts of the dead—like that of Hamlet's father —have worked upon everyone's conscience. Especially since Khrushchev's famous denunciation of Stalinism, economic improvements and political relaxation have gone hand in hand in Hungary.

Symbolic of his new tolerance, for example, is the slogan that Kadar coined a year ago for a Budapest factory audience: "He who is not against us is with us." In Kadar's earlier years—not to mention those of his hated Stalinist predecessor, Matyas Rakosi —anyone who was not actively with the regime was assumed to be against it, and soon found himself in jail. But Rakosi, after years of exile in the Soviet Union, was formally expelled from the Hungarian Communist party in 1962 in one of Kadar's gestures of de-Stalinization. And last spring under a general amnesty, nearly three thousand political prisoners were released to prepare the way for a visit by U Thant that marked the official return of Hungary to the United Nations after six years in international limbo.

The most famous victim of the suppression of the 1956 rebellion, Josef Cardinal Mindszenty, is still a prisoner in the American Legation, where he took refuge more than seven years ago. Negotiations between the Vatican and the Hungarian government for the cardinal's discreet removal seem to have been frustrated so far chiefly by the cardinal's pride. The Vatican would have removed him from the country to another post. The government, it is said, would even allow him to remain at liberty in Hungary provided he were no longer head of the country's Roman Catholic Church. But the cardinal will have none of it, insisting on the regime's capitulation to his demand that he resume his old authority. With the possible exception of the now departed Rakosi, the cardinal is perhaps the only prominent figure on either side in Hungary to have made no concessions.

The Church itself, however, has benefited from the new tolerance. Although many of its older and more militant priests are still not allowed to minister at all, religious instruction is permitted again after years of enforced suspension, and the Church receives a state subsidy.

By Western standards public criticism of the regime is muffled, restricted to officials rather than the party, to means rather than ends. But within these limits it can be sharp. Some of the complaints seem rather minuscule: ". . . the people in Hajdu need about sixty more vehicles than they have at their disposal," says a typical report. But a new press law requiring all government departments to reply to public criticism wthin two weeks has encouraged readers to deluge the newspapers with letters of complaint, sometimes uncovering sizable scandals of maladministration. "Formalism," "incompetence" and "bureaucratic action" are favorite words of editorial abuse, and party workers are constantly urged to become technically proficient instead of resorting to "slogans and appeals which, after all, cannot do the job.". . .

Translations of Western writers are commonplace items in the Budapest bookshops. Hemingway, Arthur Miller and Tennessee Williams from America; C. P. Snow, John Osborne and William Golding from Britain, stand side by side with the rebellious Russian poet Yevtushenko and the ex-prisoner Alexander Solzhenitsyn, whose bleak account of *One Day in the Life of Ivan Denisovich* shocked Moscow with the horror of Stalin's concentration camps. In the Budapest theatres Western plays seem as common as the native product. In one recent week local companies presented Shaw's *Man and Superman,* Williams's *The Glass Menagerie,* Peter Shaffer's *The Private Ear and The Public Eye* and Shakespeare's *Hamlet,* while movie theatres offered Antonioni's *La Notte* and a Peter Sellers comedy. If you are a foreigner you may obtain a Western newspaper, for the government recently authorized the porters at six of Budapest's biggest hotels to distribute on demand six papers each from six Western countries, a total daily import of just 216 copies.

Off with the Muzzle

If ordinary Hungarians are not yet trusted with foreign news, their native writers, muzzled and bullied until a year or two ago, are now less restricted than they have been since before World War II. In a country where the poets have always been rebels, this has a particular significance. Writers become barometers of the political climate, and the works issued by the state publishing house are studied eagerly for signs of a "hard" or "soft" line in state censorship. Perhaps the most convincing evidence of the new "soft" line is the rehabilitation of Tibor Dery, one of the elder statesmen of Hungarian letters. Dery was a close personal friend of Imre Nagy and was imprisoned for five years for his part in the 1956 uprising. But last year he was not only allowed to visit Britain as a guest of the British Council but was also appointed an official representative of Hungarian writers at a Moscow conference.

Still, there are restrictions at every turn. "He who is not against us is with us" is all very well, but it implies all too clearly that anyone who *is* openly against the regime had better watch out.

The security police are still powerful, although far from the ubiquitous torturers and dictators they used to be. Only since the start of this year have tenants of apartment houses been allowed to own a key to the street entrance. This enables them for the first time to let themselves in or out at night without the aid of the concierge, who has always been required in the past to report on the movements of tenants. The habits of suspicion go deep, and criticism of the regime still tends to be by innuendo and implication. Those who would like to be utterly outspoken keep their mouths shut. A young man began to talk politics with a foreign journalist one night. As soon as his cynicism began to show, his girl friend told him to shut up and dragged him away to the safety of the dance floor. A girl behind a counter wanted to live in the West where, she said, "I could make my own life, instead of having other people make it for me," but she was careful to speak only under cover of the noise of her espresso machine. She was scathing about the attitude of many of her customers. "They don't care and don't think about anything," she said. "The men are not gentlemen, and the girls just go with anybody. We're not nice here anymore, because we're not ourselves."

Most Hungarians probably would think these words exaggerated. Certainly to a foreign visitor Budapest gives the impression of being more like its historical self than it has been for a long time, relishing again a breath of freedom and a dash of style. Unlike many people elsewhere in Eastern Europe, most citizens of Budapest rarely engage in fusty proletarianism for its own sake, all open-necked shirts and dowdy print dresses. From the girl in jeans at the little café, to the elderly servant in a frayed red mess jacket who bows you into the elevator as if either he or you were the last of the Esterhazys, there is a touch of pride and panache about Budapest that is lacking in other East European capitals.

In spite of nearly twenty years of communism, four years of German occupation and a quarter of a century of political unrest before that, its people have not forgotten their inheritance. Budapest's café life, almost completely suppressed ten years ago by Rakosi, is back in full swing. Coffee and cream cakes for the ladies in the morning in Vörösmarty Square, just where the subway passengers emerge and the lottery-ticket sellers keep their sidewalk tables. Coffee and ice cream in the afternoon for the writers and artists in the ornate old Hungaria Café, among the mirrors and memories of yesterday. Snacks and chatter for students at any time in the cafés of what might be Budapest's Left Bank—but is in fact on the Danube's right bank—in the narrow alleys and sudden squares of old Buda, high above the river.

Then every night at most of the city's big restaurants there is what a visitor may regard as period musical comedy, with loving couples and happy family parties munching tirelessly through goulash, fish stew and chicken paprika, while gypsy violins screech tirelessly in their ears. For more sophisticated music lovers there is the Budapest Opera, where a sprinkling of black ties and long dresses on Saturday nights has begun this season to recall for the first time the more opulent and aristocratic days before the war. For children, simpletons or country bumpkins the haunted house, the water slide and the roller coaster still provide their venerable thrills in the Vidam Fun Park. And for the teen-agers, the frugal or the poor, there are snack bars with spaghetti and red wine at sixty cents a throw, coffee bars with juke boxes, dancing and pick-up girls, or the Communist "youth park" on the terrace of the old royal palace above the Danube, where the band plays staid old fox-trots, and the hot dogs costs only a nickel.

The royal palace itself still dominates the city, gazing down from the summit of Buda as aloof and immensely majestic as the Empress Maria Theresa who built it two hundred years ago. Beside it are the spires of the Coronation Church of King Matyas, where the rulers of Hungary were crowned for six hundred years and where country visitors, wandering up the dark Gothic aisles on weekend jaunts, still cross themselves before the disused altar. Below and beyond are the wide, curling Danube and the geometrical nineteenth century boulevards of Pest, with the baroque pinnacles of the Parliament House to remind everyone of the democracy that failed. And behind those again, leading eastward to the fun park, is the wide Avenue of the People's Republic that used to be called Stalin Avenue—until he failed too.

Often you can still see the marks of war and insurrection in bullet-pocked walls and in heavy timbers that buttress sagging gables. But much has been or is being rebuilt, including even Maria Theresa's palace, until lately so much the symbol of a reactionary past that the government refused to repair the wreckage left when the Germans made their last stand against the Russians there in 1945. For the last eight years the palace has been haunted by the ghosts of the rebels who died among its ruins after their rising failed in 1956. But now its 860 rooms are being rebuilt by the state at great cost. And as the refurbished ruins emerge, stone by glistening stone, from behind their veil of scaffolding, it is as if Hungary, too, were transforming her recent ruinous past into something more suited to her distinguished history.

Bikinis Go on Parade

It is no use pretending, however, that Budapest is some resurgent Paris of the East. It is rather more like London in 1950, just struggling out of postwar austerity, when ration books were slowly disappearing, the shop windows had begun to fill with imported luxuries, and the British for the first time in a decade glimpsed a distant prospect of prosperity. There are French perfumes and Western canned foods, cars from Poland, Russia and East Germany, and refrigerators and television sets made in Hungary. There are state hairdressing salons all over the city offering the latest thing in bouffants for fifty cents, and fashion shows of clothes from the State Design Laboratory are a daily event at the city's department stores. Boots and bikinis, ski and après-ski outfits, cocktails, dinner and long evening dresses all go down the runway.

To party diehards of the Stalinist school such prosperous frivolity seems deplorable. They prefer self-denial for its own sake, fearing that affluence will corrupt the workers, and frequent articles in the party press are devoted to dispelling their anxiety. "Today it is abundantly clear," said a characteristic piece in the chief party paper, *Nepszabadsag*, "that the raising of living standards is as much a principal process in socialist building as the consolidation of class consciousness of the masses. Motor bicycles, TV sets, refrigerators, modern furniture, household machines, decent clothes, have become the requirements of average workers. Our prosperity is the most marked expression of socialism."

While the average Hungarian income remains only about $70 a month, and a small Russian Moskvitch automobile costs $2,800 —payable in cash—there cannot be many Sunday drivers among the masses. There are still only 45,000 privately owned cars in the country (less than one for two hundred people), but this is nearly double the car ownership of two years ago and seventeen times the figure for 1957. The regime is proud of this improvement. "GAZDAGODUNK!" said one sign on a factory notice board —meaning, more or less, "We've never had it so good!" And beneath was a chart showing the number of washing machines, television sets, cars, motor bicycles and radios owned by the two thousand workers in the factory. In 1958 only two workers had owned cars and in 1960 only three. By 1962 the figure had risen to eleven, last year it soared to sixty-two, and this year according to all projections the curve of car ownership will climb off the chart.

For the first time Hungarians are enjoying the luxury of choice. It is no longer possible to sell any old rubbish just because there is nothing else. Hungarians can now buy television sets, radios and refrigerators on credit, just like their exiled cousins in the West. This practice is not yet widespread, and prices are still high for local wage earners. A 21-inch television set costs more than $300, and a small refrigerator not much less. But Hungarians are helped by the fact that both men and women normally hold jobs—children are left in state nurseries every morning —and by food-price controls and state rent subsidies.

Despite all the new apartments that surround every Hungarian town, the housing shortage is acute. Families commonly live in a single room, and share a bathroom and kitchen with another family. But the state keeps rents fixed at a few dollars a month, and now the government is cautiously experimenting with the sale of houses. Selected tenants are being offered long-term mortgages as a means of spreading some of the vast burden of capitalizing construction that until now the state has shouldered alone. "If they keep this up," said an elderly skeptic in a café, "my son may live long enough to get the family properties back again."

The entrenched power of the old Communist party diehards has been whittled away not only by wider public criticism but also by the appointment of increasing numbers of young technicians and managers qualified for their jobs by ability and training instead of by party membership. All these younger men have a pragmatic outlook that seems heretical to the suspicious old party *apparatchiks* they have succeeded. The new breed explains that the Communist party was originally a conspiracy, and its members were isolated from everyone but themselves. When at last they were victorious, they no longer knew much about ordinary life and ordinary people. "They lived in a dream world," said one young official. "We have to live with reality."

Repeatedly in Budapest offices a foreign visitor gets the impression that Hungary is seeking more room for maneuver both at the international and the individual level. . . . Nobody now feels compelled to do exactly as Moscow does. But the process had begun long before, when Khrushchev first spoke favorably about different roads to socialism, and the Hungarian people tried to test his words in practice. Unhappily for them, they went too far too fast. Khrushchev, pressed by his own diehards and harried, as we now know, by the Chinese, responded by crushing the challenge from Budapest. No doubt, seen from Moscow, the situation offered him no choice.

But time has brought its own revenge. Kadar, whose appeal was made to justify the intervention of the Red Army, has adopted many of the ideas of the rebellion it so ruthlessly put down. . . .

The Russian soldiers in Hungary, who once numbered a million, have been reduced to fifty thousand, and there are even rumors of their withdrawal if Moscow can secure some reciprocal reduction of NATO troops in the West. And throughout Eastern Europe the Communist parties are beginning, for the first time since 1945, to make significant concessions to nationalism. The old, monolithic Eastern bloc is starting to crack before our eyes.

This does not mean that communism is necessarily on the way out, but rather that flexibility is on the way in. . . .

Essentially the last eight years have forced Kadar to recognize the obvious: The majority of Hungarians are not Communists and probably never will be, and if he cannot bully them into submission, he must woo them into cooperation. "We have to work," he said a year ago, "as if there were twenty parties and secret balloting every day. That is the only way people will support us." There is, however, only one party, and there is no secret ballot. But it is a singular tribute to the tenacity and independent nature of the Hungarian people that Kadar should have made such a statement.

Ultimately this is the reward for the blood spilled eight years ago in Budapest. Not for the first time in their history, Hungarians have proved that you cannot, entirely and forever, suppress the liberties of ordinary men.

CRISIS IN CZECHOSLOVAKIA [6]

The overpowering impression in traveling through Czechoslovakia is one of unrelieved squalor. The accumulation of dirt and decay in Prague, and especially in Pilsen, is so flagrant that it seems deliberate. The scribbled signs tacked on many buildings almost sum up the situation: "Pozor, Pada Omitka" ("Beware of Falling Plaster"). Most of the Czechs I talked to were quick to apologize for this really depressing state of general disrepair. "Why don't people clean things up a bit?" I asked.

[6] From "Kafka's Nightmare Comes True," by George Bailey, correspondent for *The Reporter*. *The Reporter*. 30:15-20. My. 7, '64. Copyright 1964 by The Reporter Magazine Company. Reprinted by permission.

"Nobody cares; nothing belongs to anybody any more; everything to the state." "Then why doesn't the state clean things up?" "The state can't. It has neither the money nor the men to do the job."

A current theory has it that the Czech economy has been subtly and systematically ruined by the Good Soldier Schweik that is in every Czech—Jaroslav Hasek's folk hero, the certified idiot who is nobody's fool and whose "ingenious stupidity" foils authority at every turn. This is a myth. But there is a legitimate cause for the myth. The Czech economy has indeed been subtly and systematically sabotaged, but the real culprit is the system. The pervading neglect is categorically determined by a system of priorities designed to foster the indiscriminate expansion of basic industries. Over the past ten years the Czech government has consistently invested from 30 to 35 per cent of the national budget in the economy, mainly in the expansion of industry. Billions of dollars have been spent in building new plants and machines that are either not yet in production or have only been put into production long after construction was completed. Maintenance costs increase geometrically with plant expansion. The disregard of maintenance has disrupted services and crippled transport. It has resulted in poor quality of product and a high incidence of rejects. The Czechs lost 1.5 billion crowns (over $200 million) through rejects last year alone—an almost 12 per cent increase over 1962—and the relatively poor quality of many Czech products has caused dissatisfaction among consumers both at home and abroad. This combined with a rigid central planning system that studiously ignores consumer interests and needs, has produced a vast backlog of unsalable products. The Czechs did not vociferously complain, but they did refuse to buy. "A crucial oversight of the totalitarian state," said a Slovak writer, "is that there is no codified penalty for sales resistance." Meanwhile the ponderous, dilapidated machinery of state enterprise creaks implacably on, churning out huge quantities of outmoded or inferior articles which can never be sold or which, if any are sold, merely ensure that future Czech goods will not be.

The plan for the building and operation of power stations is far behind schedule. A shortage of electricity is the chronic anemia of all Communist states. The scanty lighting of streets gives their cities a peculiar, spectral aspect at night. In villages the blackout is almost complete. Driving from Brno to Bratislava at night, I noticed that the headlights of my car usually provided the only illumination in the streets of the villages through which I passed. "What did people use for light before candles?" runs the appropriate Czech joke. Answer: "Electricity." Here there is a direct connection between the general Communist economic failure and the policy of peaceful coexistence: the jamming of foreign radio broadcasts consumes enormous amounts of electricity. Faced with bankruptcy, each regime has been forced to choose between feeding power into productive industry or pouring it down the rathole of electronic interference. The choice throughout the bloc has been to reduce jamming. The Czech government has ceased jamming Voice of America broadcasts in English and all Austrian broadcasts. The latter clearance is particularly appreciated since many of the people speak German as a second language.

The cracks in the Czechoslovak economy began to appear as early as 1955, but the government took alarm only in 1962, when it was already too late to effect a relatively smooth correction. The year 1963 was set aside for reorganization and the drafting of a new long-term plan. Hence the production plan for last year called for an increase of only 1 per cent. Actually, total production fell 0.4 per cent below the 1962 level. To make matters worse, the new plan proved to be useless. The reverse was even more violent in some sectors of the economy. Building construction, for example, fell 10 per cent below the 1962 level. But the worst performance of all was in the construction of agricultural housing, where only 5 per cent of the plan was fulfilled. This spectacular failure was the more distressing because agriculture is the particular problem child of the economy and the agricultural construction program was designed to attract more workers to the farms. Gross agricultural production for 1962 fell 7.6

per cent below the 1961 level, which the government has so far been unable to equal.

The government became worried. In the fall of 1962, the first queues appeared in front of foodstores: food, and especially meat, had become scarce. Shortly thereafter a weekly meatless day and an antimeat propaganda campaign were introduced. "I'm going to Pilsen," says one Czech to another in Prague. "Why? Is there meat in Pilsen?" "No—that's where the end of the line is." Then came the great Soviet wheat-crop failure, which affected the entire bloc. "Have you heard," runs the current Czech anecdote, "about the latest Russian miracle? They plant wheat in the Ukraine, and it comes up in Canada!" At the same time the Chinese reduced their exports of food—including a good deal of canned meat—to the merest trickle. By 1963, trade with China, once fifth among Czech foreign clients, had virtually ceased. Worst of all, Comecon, the Soviet-bloc economic union, failed to meet its commitments to the Czechs.

Under the allocation of economic activities laid down in the Soviet grand design for the satellite countries, Czechoslovakia was to provide machines, tools, and finished products, while predominantly agricultural countries were to provide much of the food. In most cases the countries designated simply could not provide the food. Where they could, other considerations prevented the promised deliveries. For example, Comecon has had its own chicken war [just as did the United States and its Atlantic partners]: the Hungarians, who specialize in the production of chickens for export, preferred to send them to Western countries for hard currency. The Rumanians found a similar excuse for nondelivery. To make up for the resultant shortages, the Czech government has been forced to delve still further into its depleted foreign currency reserves to purchase wheat from Canada and, through European middlemen, wheat and soybeans from the United States. The Czech economy is eating its own tail.

"How Could We Have Done It?"

The greatest single problem in agriculture, as in the economy at large, is the acute manpower shortage. "Six hundred street-cleaners could clean up Prague in less than three weeks," a Czech journalist told me. "But we don't have six hundred men to spare for the job, and if we did, the government could not afford to spend so much money on a mere cleaning operation." The government does not have the skilled workers available to build new machinery or even to build new factories to house old machinery. This despite the fact that women work to a degree unheard of in Europe, including the Soviet Union. More than 43 per cent of the total labor force and 39 per cent of the industrial labor force is made up of women. Nearly half of the agricultural workers are women; in many sectors of the economy, such as transport and services, women workers form the majority. In order to live decently, both husband and wife must work. The abortion rate, the highest in Europe, in 1963 was one for every two births in Bohemia and Moravia and one for every three births in Catholic Slovakia.

The net result of this combination of circumstances ("We are operating within a context of overlapping vicious circles") has been general collapse of morale—especially in the Czech lands—and, specifically, a galloping deterioration of labor discipline. This is the theme of the daily party harangues to the public.

Sixteen years after the great experiment of Communist planning began, all are agreed that it has resulted in an almost unqualified failure. But the debacle in Czechoslovakia is not just another Communist economic failure. In Czechoslovakia, communism was put to a laboratory test under apparently ideal conditions. In 1948 the party took over an industrial society with one of the most highly skilled labor forces in the world and a plant in generally good condition. To be sure, the Soviets have exploited the country's economy in truly colonialist fashion. But the exploitation could have been intelligent. It was not. The system of exploitation used could have been resisted. It was not. "How could we," asked a prominent Czech economist rhetorically, "the most highly industrialized nation in Eastern Europe, have taken the Stalinist system of highly centralized, nonspecialized planning which sets the same broad quantitative norms for all fields of production—a system devised to increase radically the basic, heavy industrial plant of a backward nation—how could we have been so stupid as to take such a system and impose it lock, stock, and barrel on our economy? It's incredible."

For several months now a heated discussion has been in progress between old-line party stalwarts and the great majority of the country's economists over how to retrieve the economy from its present plight. This controversy is a reflection of the controversy in the arts: broadly speaking, the same groups—intellectuals against party hacks at all levels—are involved in both struggles; the basic issue is the same. What is at stake is the concept of economic centralism and hence central control by the party. . . . The hard core of the party argues . . . that to do away with centralism is to abandon socialism. The intellectuals argue that persistence in central control will inevitably bankrupt the economy in the one case and perpetuate the stagnation of the arts in the other. The ultimate problem, as the economist Oto Sik put it in a recent article, . . . is how "to incite the economic interest of our own producers"—specifically, how to spur the profit motive but pull up short of the concept of private property.

The party stalwarts, in doggedly holding the line, have been reduced for the most part to mere exhortation: "Work harder, save more, increase quality." They realize that the economy is drastically overextended. The government has recently announced its intention to close 162 enterprises before the year is out. It has prepared a vague system of material incentives— bonuses and the like for outstandingly productive and "socially useful" units and individuals—apparently to be paid out of the money saved from the dismissal of supernumeraries. Finally, it has begun a comprehensive austerity program that includes a considerable readjustment of prices (a 10 per cent increase in the price of a number of quality meat and dairy products and fish on February 10 [1964], a 10 per cent increase of all restaurant prices on April 1), wages, rents (to be raised on October 1 to cover the half-billion-crown deficit between maintenance costs and income from rental), and pensions (a general reduction). Also, the free distribution of school supplies will cease on July 1, and the distribution of free medicine sometime this year. [Most of these measures are now in effect.—Ed.] These measures amount to a fairly drastic reduction of the state's social-welfare overhead, the more painful to the public for its coming all at once—a massive blow that could easily have been avoided if the party-state had come alive to its problems seven years ago.

Even these correctives are not nearly drastic enough to effect the desired change. Not hundreds but literally thousands of enterprises are in effect working against the economy. What is called for as a start in the right direction is the massive dismantling and scrapping of obsolete and irrelevant plant. What is then needed is a basic recasting of the economy so that factories will be able to shift quickly into mass production of highly specialized goods to meet the changing consumer demands in a modern industrial society. This need is particularly pressing in view of the Common Market's scheduled fixing of united trade policies in 1965. At that time all bilateral trade agreements between members of the Market and Eastern-bloc countries will be renegotiated. If Czechoslovakia is not then in a position to meet the Market's specified needs, it will lose out.

A Warning from Comrade Ulbricht

In its search for a solution, the party has sent numerous delegations to Yugoslavia to study the system of workers' councils and, more important, the limited system of free enterprise that the Yugoslavs have gradually extended over the years (a private firm may now employ up to ten men). But these explorations are being made gingerly. The party has apparently no intention of adopting many of the Yugoslav innovations in Czechoslovakia.

So far, the most revolutionary step that the government has reluctantly taken is the campaign to attract foreign tourists on a mass scale. This development has necessitated the abolition or relaxation of a whole series of restrictions affecting Czechs as well as foreigners. Since foreign tourists are now allowed to come in, some local tourists must be allowed to go out. Here, despite severe currency restrictions and strict group-tour arrangements, the government must and does accept the inevitability of a certain amount of defection of Czech tourists. Out of approximately two hundred Czech visitors at the Olympic Winter Games in Innsbruck, eleven asked for asylum. Over the Easter weekend, three out of a busload of some forty Czechs decided to stay in the West. In both directions of the tourist flow, the regime has exposed itself to comparisons at a time when the economic situation of the country is bound to get worse. But the risk had to be taken; Czechoslovakia is in dire need of foreign exchange. Tourism is also another way to lay the foundations for better relations with the West with a view to receiving long-term credits—that is, as a means of inducing the West to finance the salvaging of the system. These credits must come primarily from America and West Germany. As regards America, this entails a restoration of most-favored-nation status and an abrogation of the strategic embargo. But West Germany is a very special case.

Last fall it was generally expected that a trade agreement involving the reciprocal establishment of official trade missions between Germany and Czechoslovakia was imminent. In October the Czechs even arranged an interview with President Antonin Novotny for the West German magazine *Der Stern,* in which he came out strongly for better relations and, specifically, more trade. Then something happened. Negotiations have been on ice ever since. . . .

The two words I heard most often in political discussion were "dilettantes" and "bunglers." In the sixteen years the Communists have been in power, they have created their own cacistocracy—the rule of the worst—and have produced collective squalor. The party demands that its leaders come from a working-class background in the strictest sense of the term. (A former chairman of the Slovakian Communist party was a tailor, another chairman was a shoemaker. "Now the one might have been a very good tailor and the other was probably a good shoemaker," said a local party secretary, "but they were both lousy chairmen.") "Obedience, blind and absolute," is another prerequisite, and a system of political commissars dictates the primacy of political control at all times and all levels. "A factory manager," a local party secretary complained, "has to contend continuously with the local factory party leader, who may be a simple worker and a dumb one at that. There is the same friction between the government and the party."

The politically active members of the party now favor radical change. However, certain members of the top leadership firmly opposed to any such change have the backing of the politically indifferent membership and the opportunists—the "loyal incompetents" spread throughout the middle echelons of factory management and planning who stand to lose their jobs in any meaningful reorganization. The spearhead of opposition to the present policies is, as usual the Academy of Sciences.

De-Stalinization was slow to reach Czechoslovakia. More than five years after Khrushchev's 20th Party Congress speech in 1956 —long after their Polish and Hungarian neighbors had tumultuously and more or less thoroughly de-Stalinized—the Czech Communists began making the first cautious moves toward cleaning out their own Augean stables, and then only under Soviet pressure. There were compelling reasons for this reluctance: unlike any other Communist country, Czechoslovakia is a dual-nation state. There are striking differences between Czechs and Slovaks in language, history, culture, and temperament, and the Stalinist purge in Czechoslovakia was conducted largely along discriminatory, nationalist lines. During the Second World War the Czech lands were included in the Third Reich as a protectorate; Slovakia was a so-called autonomous state. More important, while the Czechs were effectively forced to drudge in support of the German war machine, the Slovaks made use of their special situation and highly suitable terrain to mount a considerable partisan movement under Communist leadership. The Slovaks claim to have had a hundred thousand men under arms in the mountains in 1944. In short, the Slovaks possess a partisan tradition, while the Czechs have the tradition of obedience under the book, a tradition hardly the less onerous for being historically and geographically understandable.

When the Soviet Army finally "liberated" most of Czechoslovakia in 1945, it brought with it the cadre of the Czech Communist party from its exile in Russia. The friction between the old Communist exiles centered in Prague and the young Communist partisans headquartered in the Slovak capital, Bratislava, began immediately. When the purging season came, the Czechs condemned the Slovak Communist leaders on charges of "bourgeois nationalism." With their recent rehabilitation and the party's admission that the charges against them were trumped up, the Slovak cause has become identified with the general campaign for reform. Also, the Slovak drive for equality (not autonomy) and the general drive against artistic, economic, and administrative centralized control thus neatly coincide, since the center under attack in both cases is Prague.

Under increasing pressure from the intellectuals, the regime first jettisoned Karol Bacilek, first secretary of the Slovak Communist party, and then last September Premier Viliam Siroky and his clique. Siroky was replaced by a Slovak, Jozef Lenart, who is generally regarded as a liberal. President Novotny, who is also first secretary of the party, is regarded as the chief holdover from the Stalinist days, and de-Stalinization cannot be considered complete until he departs.

The recent establishment of ideological commissions to improve and intensify "party guidance" of chief editors and editorial boards has so far had no visible effects. The cacistocracy is simply unable to cope with the intellectuals outside the confines of party organization. Coercion having been outlawed, at least for a time, the only effective weapon remaining to the leadership is administrative control. The leadership can and does restrict publication of intellectuals' magazines, newspapers, and books by pleading paper shortages. The embargo against all non-Communist publications from abroad is still rigorously enforced. And, of course, the regime still controls appointments and can prevent individual intellectuals from visiting ideological danger spots abroad. (Apparently, the Soviet Union has also declared Paris "off limits" to its writers: over last winter not one Soviet writer—as distinct from cultural functionaries—visited Paris.) It is more difficult to restrict travel within the bloc without openly declaring a state of hostilities: the Czech critic Antonin Liehm scooted down to Budapest in January and came back with an interview supporting complete freedom of expression from the grand old man of Marxist letters, George Lukacs (during his imprisonment with Imre Nagy, Lukacs had decided that Kafka's *The Trial* is a realistic novel).

In some ways the party has been strengthened by the revolt; it might not even have survived without it. Avowedly, the intellectuals are trying desperately to rehabilitate Marxism, to develop a philosophical product that makes sense. They regard their attempt as the only means of countering a precipitate, general loss of faith—a loss that is most conspicuous among the youth of the country.

"Every one of the young people I know in the theatre," a director told me, "is violently anti-Communist—and often enough for the wrong reasons." There is vague hope, and more often mere resignation to the idea that some form of socialism can be worked out. A good many writers would like to be Marxists; a good many more would like not to have been Marxists in vain. In Marxist terms, there is an interrelationship between a society's economic base and its cultural superstructure—between the factory and the theatre. The Czechs have discovered from experience that they do not know what this connection is. Whatever it is, the writers demand relative autonomy. They suspect that the best way to make the connection between the economic base and the cultural superstructure active is to do the work the superstructure demands.

CZECHS REVAMPING ECONOMIC SYSTEM [7]

Czechoslovakia has begun a radical overhaul of her entire economic system that is certain to produce profound though gradual political changes as well.

Under pressure of a severe economic slump and after the failure of other liberal economic reforms, the government has now decreed a total assault upon planning and management techniques developed in the Soviet Union and long held to be synonymous with communism itself.

The economic vocabulary of Soviet-style Marxism is being completely redefined. So are relations between the ruling Communist party and government ministries, producers and consumers, managers and workers.

As now envisioned, central planning will consist of little more than predicting market and production opportunities here and abroad and choosing among major trends of possible development.

Large factories and trusts made up of smaller producers will direct their own affairs, negotiate many of their own prices with supplier and buyers, set their own wages above prescribed minimums and otherwise benefit or suffer from profits and losses incurred in competition with other domestic and foreign producers.

The basic new management principles were adopted . . . after months of bitter debate in party and government organs. They go far beyond tentative experiments in the Soviet Union and the adoption of some similar ideas in Hungary and Poland, officials say. . . .

The party's ratification of the new system was the culmination of eight years of work. In the last six months [during the second half of 1964] the economists overcame the last-ditch objections of conservatives in the party and industry who feared loss of control over the economy. In the end the party's central committee is said to have agreed by a large majority to introduce the new system gradually but "forthwith," and in time to make it the basis of the long-term plan for 1966-70.

[7] From article by Max Frankel, New York *Times* correspondent. New York *Times*. p 1+. N. 6, '64. © 1964 by the New York Times Company. Reprinted by permission.

Commissions Begin Work

Special commissions, with the young economists well represented on the central bodies, have begun to translate the principles
into guidelines for new methods of determining wages, prices,
rents, taxes, credits, interest dates, foreign and retail trade policies
and methods of conducting decentralized transactions and labor
relations. . . .

The over-all change, economists predict, will force Czechoslovakia to specialize in the production of goods that she and the
world can consume.

The new system is expected greatly to enhance the political
influence here of the ablest managers of industry and the ablest
representatives of workers' organizations. Important political ad-
justments are thus expected in Czechoslovakia and in her relations
with the rest of the world.

The principal impetus for the adoption of the new system—
and the reduction of central controls over other aspects of life
here—has been the state of Czechoslovakia's economy in recent
years. The volume of industrial production last year fell below
the poor 1962 level. Labor productivity and national income have
remained static.

Since Czechoslovakia has long been recognized as the most
advanced industrial country in the Communist world, economists
began to challenge not only management techniques but also the
basic assumptions of Communist economic theory.

Resources Squandered

Through centralized planning and control, resources were
squandered on almost every imaginable industrial product—from
airplanes to xylophones. This overextension produced intolerably
high costs of production, manpower shortages and, above all, a
loss of quality in comparison with the products of more-special-
ized competitors. Prague was forced to sell cheaply abroad and
the cost of living . . . soared.

There was no way to reverse the trend because central planning of production could control only quantity, not quality. It

could not enforce technological improvement, innovation and refinement, which depend upon the producer's interest in his goods. What is more, the race for rewards for greater quantities of production further damaged quality. The system often punished those interested most in efficiency.

The essence of the new system is to replace the interest of enterprises in meeting fixed production quotas with an interest in promoting their own profits.

These profits will not be, as in parts of the Hungarian and other Communist countries' economies, merely another centrally determined quantitative unit of measuring performance but . . . "a true outcome of enterprise economy."

Many officials were willing to accept the notion of profits as a unit of measurement but without releasing total control over wages, prices and other elements of actual income. That is the battle that the economists have now won. They also overcame what they called the "ideological prejudice" that market influences and price and wage fluctuations are incompatible with "Socialist planning."

As the party decree put it: "What is beneficial to society must be beneficial to the enterprise and to the individual. Good work will be rewarded; dead work will not be paid for as it has been to date."

It established the following principles:

Price policies will reward technical innovation and depreciation policies will encourage the abandonment of outmoded techniques. Research and development programs will be geared to long-term plans and investments, but individual enterprises will be free to contract for research.

Investment in basic development projects will be centrally planned on the advice of larger enterprises and export managers and will be financed from the state budget. Enterprises and trusts will also be allowed to modernize or rationalize production by investing their profits or drawing bank credits on fixed terms. General overhauls will be financed by enterprises from depreciation accounts.

For the first time enterprises will be charged not only depreciation rates but also interest on those rates at differentiated terms.

Foreign trade will be reorganized by commodity groups. Enterprises using imported raw materials will have to take into account their real costs. Experiments will be used to determine whether certain enterprises can in effect manage their own foreign trade.

All wages and bonuses are to be paid from net income. Receipts from sales will be used to pay for materials, power, transport and depreciation, leaving a gross income for the payment of interest and taxes and for investments. What remains will have to cover minimum wages, allowances and bonuses.

Enterprises will be allowed to reduce their work forces. Unprofitable enterprises will be subsidized for only limited periods.

Price ceilings and competing foreign products will be used to check efforts to raise prices faster than productivity.

Prices are to reflect production costs and, with some reservations, the relation between supply and demand. They will reward technical advance and higher quality and will be influenced to some extent by world market prices.

Basic raw materials, power and basic foodstuffs will be sold at centrally fixed prices. Other goods will be subject to maximum and perhaps minimum price limits and an increasing number of goods will be sold at terms negotiated by suppliers and customers or, in retail trade, at terms selected by retail organizations with a view to supply and demand.

THE AFFAIR OF THE POLISH INTELLECTUALS [8]

When thirty-four prominent Polish intellectuals wrote a letter last March [1964] to Premier Cyrankiewicz protesting against censorship, it turned out to be the most important political event in Poland since 1956. The protest brought a painful setback to those who have been pressing for tighter cultural policies. It faced

[8] From article in *East Europe*. 13:34-7. Je. '64. Reprinted by permission.

Gomulka and the government with a difficult decision: whether to disregard the letter and risk passive resistance from the nation's intellectuals, or to promise them that the constitutional guarantees of cultural freedom would be more closely respected.

The authorities at first took punitive measures, but protests from the West forced them to reconsider. Like the Stalinists of the past, they then sought to convict the Western press and radio of attempting to "blow the whole matter up, and present it in a false light in the international forum.". . .

Following is a chronology of the main events surrounding the letter.

December. Jaroslaw Iwaszkiewicz, chairman of the Union of Polish Writers, complained in an open letter of inadequate allotments of paper for periodicals and books. . . .

January. Complaints of writers about inadequate paper allotments and strict censorship "were voiced at a Polish Writers Union meeting, but no relief was granted."

March. The same complaints were voiced again at a meeting between a group of intellectuals and Wincenty Krasko, chief of the Cultural Department of the Central Committee, but to no avail. The decision was then made to send a letter to Premier Cyrankiewicz.

March 14. Thirty-four prominent intellectuals signed a letter of complaint addressed to Premier Cyrankiewicz. The undersigned demanded that "Polish cultural policy be changed to conform to the spirit of the rights guaranteed by the Polish Constitution and for the good of the nation."

March 19. Antoni Slonimski, a well-known poet and former chairman of the Writers Union, personally delivered the letter of protest to the office of Cyrankiewicz.

March 26. Reuters and UPI carried the first reports of the letter and the reprisals which followed it. Radio Free Europe mentioned the letter for the first time in a broadcast based on the Reuters report.

March 27. The security police arrested and questioned Jan Jozef Lipski, former secretary of the Crooked Circle Club in Warsaw, "suspected of having collected signatures for the letter."

April 1. Western newspapers and UPI reported that J. J. Lipski had been arrested . . . but released within 48 hours. . . .

April 8. A meeting between some of the signers of the letter and Premier Cyrankiewicz took place in Warsaw.

April 13. The passport of Jan Kott, distinguished critic and Shakespearean scholar, was confiscated so that he was unable to deliver an April 18 lecture in Paris.

April 14. The newsprint allotment of the Cracow Catholic weekly, *Tygodnik Powszechny,* was cut by 25 per cent. . . . Editor-in-chief Jerzy Turowicz . . . [had] signed the letter of protest.

The satirical weekly *Szpilki* (Warsaw) dropped one of its weekly features: Antoni Slonimski's feuilleton.

An Italian newspaper reported a "solidarity movement among Polish students and printers" in support of the Polish intellectuals. The daily added that the intellectuals who signed the letter were blacklisted by the regime.

April 19. Warsaw printing workers were reported to have told the Polish authorities that they would go on strike if any of the thirty-four writers banned by Mr. Gomulka is arrested. . . .

April 30. In the United States House of Representatives, Representative Clement J. Zablocki, a Wisconsin Democrat and member of the House Foreign Affairs Committee, said that a reassessment of U.S. policy toward Poland might be required if the Polish government took any further action against Polish intellectuals.

May 1. The International Federation of Free Journalists issued a protest to UN Secretary General U Thant against the "censorship and growing restrictions of intellectual freedom in Poland." The Federation asked U Thant and the UN to press the Polish government to cease "restrictions, persecution and pressures on Polish intellectuals."

May 3. British correspondent Christopher Russel wrote: "The Communist leaders of Poland moved with remarkable speed to correct the unfortunate impression created in the West by their rough treatment of the thirty-four writers and scholars who protested against censorship.". . .

May 10. A Warsaw daily . . . printed a letter signed by 150 writers . . . protesting the "organized campaign" led by the Western press . . . and . . . "foreign interference in our internal problems and . . . cultural policy." . . .

May 14. [Two] newspapers . . . published a list of 233 "additional" writers and "representatives of Polish literature" who wished to protest along with those whose names were published on May 10.

May 15. Jan Kott, . . . was permitted to visit Vienna where he was one of the recipients of the 1964 Herder Prize. . . .

May 17. Jaroslaw Iwaszkiewicz, chairman of the Polish Writers Union, announced in a newspaper interview that the authorities had increased the paper allotment for publishing, granted higher pay for writers, and authorized the publication of one or two new literary periodicals.

POLAND'S UNEMPLOYMENT PROBLEM [9]

Marxists have always claimed that the phenomenon of unemployment is an inherent evil of the capitalist economy. Only the nationalization of industry, transport and trade, and the establishment of a planned economy, they have argued, can ensure a rate of economic growth which will guarantee work to everyone. Idle productive capacity and unemployed manpower were thought to be twin symbols of the wastefulness of the capitalist system. Thus the existence of serious unemployment in Poland is embarrassing from the ideological standpoint as well as for the usual social and personal reasons.

The fact is that hundreds of thousands of Polish workers now face the prospect of long-term unemployment. Mass layoffs are under way in factories and offices all around the country. So-called redundancy commissions are busy in all branches of industry, and the government has virtually prohibited any new hirings until the middle of this year. But even when the job freeze is lifted, new opportunities will be severely limited. It is officially stated in Warsaw that the growth of total employment

[9] From article by Michael Gamarnikow, an economist specializing in Soviet affairs. *East Europe.* 13:30-3. Je. '64. Reprinted by permission.

will be kept down to some 100,000 annually, not only in 1964 but for another two or three years at least. Consequently, both the employees dismissed during the current redundancy drive, and the young people entering the labor market in the 1964-1966 period, will find it increasingly difficult to secure jobs. A high rate of residual unemployment is likely to persist at least until the end of 1966.

But the situation is bad enough now. In its issue of March 20, the mass-circulation paper *Zycie Warszawy* printed a few of "many letters" arriving daily at its editorial office. "Are there any chances of finding employment for personnel dismissed from drafting offices?" an architect asked. A skilled plumber wrote: "I shall take my family and go wherever I can find work and housing." These are the problems of highly skilled workers in Poland after twenty years of Communist planning. . . .

Nobody knows how many people will be ultimately affected, since the targets of the redundancy drive were never made public. There is a rumor in Warsaw that the Central Committee has decided upon a straight 10 per cent across-the-board slash in the socialized sector of the economy. This seems likely to prove an exaggeration. But according to the best available estimates, between 100,000 and 150,000 people can be expected to lose their jobs during 1964. According to figures published in *Trybuna Ludu*, April 29, and in *Biuletyn Statystyczny*, December 1963, total employment in the socialized sector decreased by 350,000 between the end of October and the end of February. While 150,000 of this may be taken as seasonal variation in the working force, the remaining 200,000 seem to represent the net effect of the redundancy drive. Some of those people may eventually be retired, but a substantial number are likely to remain jobless.

The exact figures for total unemployment may never be known. Although Poland is the only Communist country that publishes unemployment statistics, official sources have admitted that the figures are far from complete. Because there are no unemployment benefits, and because the local employment offices have little to offer other than the most menial jobs mainly on state farms, only a small percentage of the unemployed bother to register.

The leading Polish economic weekly estimated some time ago that in order to arrive at the actual number of unemployed in Poland one would have to multiply the official figures by five. On this basis one can estimate that at the end of 1963 there must have been over 300,000 unemployed.

In addition, as we have already mentioned, some 100,000-150,000 people are likely to lose their jobs during 1964, while 175,000 juveniles are officially expected to enter the labor market. Even with the permitted annual increase in the labor force of 100,000 and the jobs made available by death and retirement, the number of unemployed in Poland at the end of 1964 can be expected to reach 450,000. This amounts to over 5 per cent of the total labor force of 8.5 million people—a very high figure given Poland's economic condition.

It is important to bear in mind that the standard of living of the average Polish working-class family depends primarily on the number of its breadwinners. Even if nobody who is the sole provider for his family is laid off, as the official guidelines stipulate, the standard of living of tens of thousands of families will be drastically reduced because of the loss of additional earnings. And since at least two employed people per family are needed to balance the average working-class budget, thousands of families may be pushed beyond the borderline of real poverty. This explains the wave of anxiety, verging on near panic, which the mass layoffs have provoked in Poland.

EAST GERMANY: SKETCH OF A SATELLITE [10]

Superficially, the political evolution of East Germany has paralleled that of West Germany. The Soviet occupation authorities set up the German Democratic Republic in 1949 soon after the Federal Republic was established. In 1955 after West Germany had acquired its sovereignty, the Russians extended "soverignty" to East Germany; and shortly after Bonn's ac-

[10] From *Great Decisions 1965.* (Fact Sheet no 2. Germany—Key to Europe?) Foreign Policy Association. 345 E. 46th St. New York, N.Y. 10017. '65. p 21. Copyright 1965 by the Foreign Policy Association, Inc. Reprinted by permission.

ceptance into NATO, East Germany became a member of the Warsaw pact (Moscow's Eastern European response to NATO).

Here any parallel ends. West Germany is a democracy and East Germany is a totalitarian dictatorship. Its democratic trappings—an elected government and a multiparty system—are trappings and no more. In 1946 the Russians experimented with free local and state elections, but their hopes were dashed by the results when their candidates failed to win the expected vote. There have been no free elections in East Germany since then. Only one of the three existing political parties has any real power: the Socialist Unity party (SED). Despite its name, the SED is Communist-run and controls every facet of East German life.

East Germany's no. 1 Communist is party chief and chairman of the Council of State, seventy-one-year-old Walter Ulbricht. He has the dubious distinction of being one of the most despised leaders in Eastern Europe and one of the few old-time Stalinists. Whereas most of the Eastern European governments have begun to display some freedom from Moscow's control, East Germany still remains a more or less obedient satellite, and Ulbricht's power largely depends on the bayonets of the twenty Soviet occupation divisions stationed in his country.

Between 1949 and mid-1961, when East Germany erected the Berlin wall, four million of its citizens fled to the West. The high watermark was reached in 1953. That was the year when unarmed East Germans revolted and were gunned down by Soviet troops.

The exodus was not only a source of acute embarrassment to the regime; it siphoned off the cream of the population—skilled workers, technicians, teachers, doctors and other professionals—and created a labor shortage which slowed down the pace of economic reconstruction. Other factors, too, handicapped postwar recovery: East Germany supplied a major proportion of Germany's reparations to Russia.

Not until 1954 did East Germany attain the equivalent of its prewar production level. By 1957 its GNP [gross national product] was only 20 per cent above the 1936 level, compared to a 90 per cent increase in West Germany. Moreover, consumers received a much smaller share of the GNP than did consumers in the Federal Republic. In imitation of the Soviet pattern, the East German economy concentrated upon the field of heavy industry. In 1958 the government suspended rationing of consumer goods and the situation began to look more promising. But then the Ulbricht regime encountered stormy seas. Economic growth declined from 12.4 per cent in 1959 to 6.2 in 1961 (the growth rate is still among the lowest in Eastern Europe). In 1963 the regime abandoned as a failure its ambitious seven-year plan (1959-65) and adopted a variety of emergency measures to revive the economy, including reorganization of its system of industrial management and provision of greater incentives to peasants and workers. These efforts, abetted by Soviet aid, appear to have borne fruits in the last year or so.

Although there are currently signs of a mild internal liberalization, East Germany remains a country where farmers have been collectivized; the middle class has virtually disappeared; and artists and writers are largely servants of the state. The mood of many East Germans is revealed in this joke which has circulated widely within the country.

Question: What should we do if the border with West Germany were to be opened?

Answer: Climb the nearest tree to escape being crushed in the stampede.

EAST GERMANY: QUIET REVIVAL [11]

Behind the wall, East Germany has been undergoing a silent economic revolution. The nation that was once grim and poverty-stricken is still grim . . . but its poverty is disappearing. With a growth rate in the first six months of the year (1964) said to be 8 per cent, East Germany makes claims to rapidly becoming an industrial power to be reckoned with. . . .

[11] From article by Kenneth Ames, *Newsweek* correspondent. *Newsweek.* 64:46-7. N. 23, '64. Reprinted by permission.

In industry, the stress is placed on quality. As one official put it: "Our goods have to be as good as West German, American, and British products to compete in a world market and that is what we are aiming for. . . . We need the foreign currency for imports and we have to earn it with our own products. We are urging people to take a close look at the quality.". . .

As a member of Comecon (the Communist version of the Common Market), East Germany is being made the Soviet bloc's center for machine-tool production, chemicals, and petrochemicals. The recent opening of the Communist bloc's oil pipeline stretching from Russia's Baku oil fields to the Oder River created a major revolution in the petrochemical and ancillary industries. Already new industrial complexes have sprung up close to the Polish border in the areas around Schwedt, the German terminus of the pipeline. . . .

Up in Rostock on the Baltic Sea coast, the shipbuilding yards are working at maximum capacity, turning out ships ranging in size from 10,000 to 15,000 tons. Their prices are competitive with the world market so that at present four of the ships under construction are for foreign shipping lines. . . .

Before the silent revolution, expensive industrial machinery was used for only eight hours a day, but now three shifts are the rule. "After all," said one party official, sounding rather like a Western businessman, "no capitalist manager or industrial magnate would dream of having his valuable equipment lying idle for more than the absolute minimum. Otherwise the machinery would never amortize itself. We have adopted the same methods and everyone is much happier, working harder, and earning more money for more work."

The better times are most immediately visible in the major cities. There is no shortage of foodstuffs with the exception of citrus fruits, which are unheard of, and butter, which is rationed. High-quality clothes are expensive but are obtainable, and the audience at the theatre is indistinguishable from similar audiences in West Germany. The air of hopelessness which was everywhere four years ago has been modified, chiefly because East Germans have suddenly discovered that their wages buy goods. "We are still short of some household things like soap powder and kitchen equipment". . . [said one East German woman]. "But after we have gone so long without being able to get anything, these are small problems."

Nonetheless there is still a definite air of depression, particularly in the major cities where for block after block there is rubble left over from World War II bombing raids. Occasionally, however, the sober view is broken by new blocks of apartment houses sprouting from the ruins, and in the rural areas new industrial complexes have been established. The apartments, though cramped, are adequate and rents are absurdly low ($9 a month for two small rooms, a kitchen, and bathroom). . . .

With the industrial output of Communist East Germany seemingly rising, it remains to be seen what the significance of this growth will be on the regime's future relations with the Soviet bloc and the West. But the Communist world certainly will not be able to ignore the radical changes, and the West, as well, might be in for some rethinking of its policy.

BULGARIA TRIES NEW DIRECTIONS [12]

This Balkan country started its third decade of Communist rule with indications of new directions in the national economy and foreign policy.

Following the examples in Hungary, the Soviet Union and Czechoslovakia, the Bulgarian leadership seems interested in revising its economic management system, hitherto highly centralized. For more than six months, experiments have been under way in various enterprises, aimed at introducing certain aspects of profit into cost accounting and at encouraging planning at the factory level. Such measures, which would increase factories' autonomy, and a form of competition between them, have been lacking in Bulgaria. So far the government of Premier Todor Zhivkov has not committed itself to clear-cut reforms. It would

[12] From Bulgaria Trying New Directions," by David Binder, New York *Times* correspondent. New York *Times*. p 25. S. 20, '64. © 1964 by The New York Times Company. Reprinted by permission.

seem that the experiments are still the subject of rivalries between party "modernists" and the "centralists" of the Stalin tradition.

In foreign affairs it is becoming clear that Sofia wants to overcome the twenty years of self-imposed isolation that made Bulgaria hostile to her neighbors, Turkey and Yugoslavia. The change started about eighteen months ago when the Bulgarians began making overtures to Yugoslavia. Since then economic and cultural relations have improved, though political relations have lagged.

The most dramatic alteration, however, has come in relations with Greece. Since the July 9 signing of twelve agreements, the two governments have been rapidly moving to restore to a normal status communications, trade and air, rail and road transport. . . .

Now it appears that Mr. Zhivkov wants to better his relations with Turkey as well. The Bulgarian press has been carrying long articles about government benefits accorded the 500,000 Turks living in Bulgaria. In his speech to the National Assembly commemorating twenty years of Communist rule, Premier Zhivkov made a warm gesture to the Turkish government. "There has been a certain improvement in our relations with our neighbor Turkey in recent years," he said, "but all has not been done in this respect as yet. We consider that there are no obstacles to making new steps forward. On behalf of the Bulgarian Government I can declare that we will continue to do all in our power for our mutual relations with neighboring Turkey."

Nevertheless, the principal emphasis in Bulgarian foreign policy is on intimate ties to the Soviet Union, which is referred to by Bulgarian officials as "our sun and our love." About 54 per cent of Bulgaria's trade is with the Soviet Union. This year Sofia got Soviet loans valued at 530 million rubles ($535.3 million). In 1963, for instance, Bulgaria exported 8,606 electric trucks and 6,000 of these went to the Soviet Union. As for imports, Bulgaria has received 90 per cent of her tractors and 70 per cent of her trucks from the Soviet Union. Moscow has built 120 factories in Bulgaria and is committed to build more.

The visitor to Bulgaria finds undeniable progress, especially in education and health services. Where there were once more than a million illiterates, today virtually every Bulgarian can read. With 98 students for every 10,000 citizens. Bulgaria contends that she ranks third behind the United States and the Soviet Union in the number of people attending universities.

The Communist regime has also built 600,000 dwellings and brought electricity to 4,700 of Bulgaria's 5,000 villages.

But its continuing industrial crash program is being paid for by ordinary citizens by sacrifices of creature comforts and consumer goods. And police control is tighter than in most countries of Eastern Europe.

ALBANIA TODAY [13]

The Communists proclaim that they now have collectivized more than 90 per cent of the farms, which anyway include more, rocks than productive land. Yet they have not changed the pre-Communist situation which enabled Albania to grow at best enough food for eight months of the year. Whatever improvements have resulted from recent farm reclamation, irrigation, and mechanization have been canceled out by the population growth.

In 1944 the population was one million; now it has almost doubled. During this period Tirana has grown from 32,000 to a metropolis of more than 152,000.

Farm production has been further impeded by the utilization of the best areas for industrial and export commodities, such as cotton, sugar, olives, grapes, and citrus fruits. Consequently while 45 per cent of the work force is engaged in agriculture Albania is still a land of food shortages.

Albanian news media assert and recent tourists confirm that consumer goods are now ample, but few Albanians can afford the high prices.

[13] From "Albanian Reds as Stern as Ever," by G. M. Panarity, writer, *Christian Science Monitor.* p 1+. N. 12, '64. Reprinted by permission from *The Christian Science Monitor.* © 1964 The Christian Science Publishing Society. All rights reserved.

The average common laborer receives less than the equivalent of a dollar a day; professionals, such as doctors, teachers, and engineers, earn about $52 a month. A suit of men's clothes costs between $140 and $152, and a laborer would have to tighten his belt for six months in order to afford one.

Visitors Cautioned

Albanian tourists visiting their native land are cautioned by friends and relatives not to wear expensive clothes during their stay in the country. One young woman who changed her dress daily was politely asked to leave on the next plane.

Rent is negligible for the fortunate few who have an apartment.

The regime's claim that Albania is no longer an agricultural but an industrial-agricultural nation has substance. During the first decade of five-year plans—ending in 1960—an incipient industry has been created using more than 45 per cent of the work force. The current five-year plan—to December, 1965—purports "to raise the living standard 55 per cent above that of 1960" by the creation of some 64 new industries and the expansion of those already in operation.

In Tirana alone, next to a textile plant employing five thousand hands are such industries as brick, glass and shoe factories, a brewery, a food processing plant, a prefabricated building materials factory, and a hydro-electric station. Similarly towns such as Durazzo, Elbasan, Korcha, Berat, Fier, Valona, and Scutari each have industrial plants.

Albania's hitherto untapped mineral wealth is also being exploited. Two of its most important cash exports are petroleum and chromium. It is said that in petroleum Albania is second to Rumania.

Albania lacks both trained technicians and, since its rift with Moscow in 1961, new machinery as well as repair parts. Communist China has been profuse in promises but slow in delivery.

Moreover Albania is plagued by a trade imbalance. Among its exports citrus fruits and olives find a ready market in the satellite countries. The regime is pressing hard to increase the production of such cash crops in order to increase exports and improve the trade balance.

Literacy Leap Boosted

The most significant progress has been in education. In 1944 illiteracy was as high as 85 per cent. The regime asserts that today every person under forty years has learned to read and write.

Early last September [1964] the Minister of Education and Culture, Manush Myfitu, declared 450,000 students were enrolled in the nation's schools, including some four thousand at the State University of Tirana. All education is free and compulsory between the ages of six and fourteen. Every village is provided with an elementary school.

Book publishing is keeping pace with the phenomenal increase in literacy. According to an American authority over 7.5 million copies of seven hundred different titles were published in 1952 alone. Much of this literary outpouring, as would be expected, is permeated with Communist propaganda.

No Crime News

A study of the Albanian Communist press shows nothing on the subjects of crime, sex, or corruption. The picture painted is one of total transformation within two decades. The world is asked to believe that what was one of the most lawless nations in Europe is now composed only of model citizens. Movies, of course, are carefully censored and no American movies are permitted.

To all appearances the regime is pretty much accepted by the younger generation. Officials say Albania is a nation of "youngsters," with those under fifteen years comprising 41 per cent of the total. Half the population has been educated under Communist rule.

The three leaders since 1954 also are relatively young. Enver Hoxha, called the "little Balkan Stalin" turned fifty-six in October. Premier Mehmed Schehu will be fifty-two next January, while Foreign Minister Behar Shtylla, a protégé of Mr. Hoxha, is forty-six. All of them have a middle-class background, and none has ever worked with his hands for a living.

The regime says that more than fifty thousand youth are party members. Out of this number ten thousand hard-core Communists are enrolled in the dreaded "Sigurimi" (Secret Police), guardians of the regime.

Since 1961 Albania's foreign policy has been Peking-oriented. At this time the regime became disillusioned first with Yugoslavia and then with the Soviet Union.

The switch from the two Slav nations to China has increased the prestige of Mr. Hoxha. His careful maneuvering is believed to have saved the country from becoming the seventh republic of federated Yugoslavia. Today Chinese technicians and artisans are very much in evidence in all principal towns. Albanian news media hailed the Chinese detonation of the nuclear device with great jubilation.

Albania now has diplomatic relations with more than a score of newly emerged Afro-Asian countries, as well as with the three NATO powers—Italy, France, and Turkey. With Italy the bitter memories of 1939 [when the Italians invaded Albania] still linger on. Up to recently, relations with France had been correct and cool, but since France established diplomatic relations with Peking, they have grown much warmer.

TITOISM IN FLUX [14]

One must have a good deal of sympathy for the American reader who tries to keep abreast of developments in Yugoslavia. Having been advised after the war that Yugoslavia was a model Soviet-type police state, he learned in 1948 that Stalin excommunicated Tito because he was not a good Communist and that Tito denounced the U.S.S.R. as a dictatorship. While pondering reports that Yugoslavia had devised a decentralized and more

[14] From article by Fred Warner Neal, head of the International Relations Program, Claremont (Calif.) Graduate School. *Current History.* 44:294-8+. My. '63. Reprinted by permission.

democratic brand of communism which we were aiding economically and militarily, he found that Milovan Djilas, the chief advocate of decentralization and democracy, was put in jail and Tito and Khrushchev were friends again. He then saw reports that the Yugoslav economic system was further decentralized and had achieved great results, only to hear a year later of economic stagnation and the tightening of controls. As if this were not enough to confuse the American reader, his newspapers then told him first, that Tito had defended Soviet nuclear testing and attacked the West, and, second, that Communist China denounced Yugoslavia as a tool of the imperialists.

Despite the well-known peccadilloes of American journalism, by and large all these conflicting reports were correct. Since the war, Yugoslavia has been in a constant state of flux, politically and economically, domestically and internationally. Yet, paradoxically, there has been at the same time—since about 1950—a certain stability and even continuity which the headlines have not always reflected.

The major elements of Titoism seem relatively fixed. Externally there is Communist nationalism and independence from the Soviet Union. Internally there is a decentralized economic system in which autonomous, worker-managed enterprises, with few direct government controls, compete in a reasonably free market economy guided more by the law of supply and demand than by planning decrees. Agriculture has been decollectivized, although a new type of cooperative increasingly spurs cooperation among the private peasants, who comprise most of the farm population. The Communist party has a monopoly of political power, but its voice has been muted as a result of greatly increased personal freedom, autonomy in local government and a nation-wide system of "direct democracy" in which more and more citizens participate in public decisions. (Locally elected and locally financed school districts, not unlike those in the United States, are an example of the latter.)

This Titoist system has by no means persuaded all Yugoslavs to become Communists. However, there is general recognition that the regime—in part because of its system and in part in spite of it—has achieved notable successes, even if economic viability cannot yet be numbered among them. The standard of living has been boosted spectacularly from the depths of postwar poverty, and underdeveloped regions once more Near Eastern than European in appearance have been built up. The basis for industrialization of a backward agricultural society has been completed. The nationalities question has not been solved, but for the first time in Yugoslav history there is a national unity in which fratricidal conflict is not a danger.

Given these achievements, one may say that the zig-zagging of Yugoslav policies at home and abroad reflects experimentation and uncertainty more than crises. But the difference is not always easy to see, and the constancy of the pendulum effect poses the question of whether it is a temporary phenomenon or is inherent in the nature of Titoism.

Titoism

To understand the Yugoslav kaleidoscope and its significance, one must focus on the factors that set off Tito's regime from other Communist countries in Eastern Europe. First, Yugoslav communism came into being under its own steam rather than as a reflection of Soviet will and power. Although they were not dependent on Moscow like their comrades elsewhere, the Yugoslav Communists considered themselves faithful Muscovites, the most faithful of the faithful. When they demurred at Soviet efforts at economic and political domination and Stalin read them out of the international Communist movement, they underwent a deep psychological trauma. This forced and produced new interpretations of Marxism which led Tito and his aides to see themselves, the Soviet Union, communism and the world in a new light. And from this emerged their unique system which more than anything else pried open the Pandora's box of Communist nationalism.

In their new guise, the Yugoslav Communists espoused a neutralist foreign policy that was at first pro-Western, in considerable part because of Soviet hostility on the one hand, and large United States handouts on the other. Yet, as Tito kept reminding the West, he and his followers were Communists and not Western-type democrats, despite the appearances of some aspects of political democracy in their system. Not only was the scorn of the rest of the Communist world hard to take, but Yugoslavs—Tito especially—had a strong yearning for Communist solidarity if it could be accomplished without giving up independence.

All this meant that Titoism had to try to maintain several positions which appear to be mutually contradictory, viz:

1. A decentralized, market economy and a planned Socialist system.

2. Political freedom and a Communist party monopoly on political power.

3. National independence, with a neutralist foreign policy, and efforts at solidarity with the Moscow-led Commuunist bloc.

The Yugoslav national disinclination to practice restraint and moderation has aggravated the problem of finding a balance. Initial decentralization in the early 1950's came too fast and went too far. Despite the skeptics' doubts, factories really were turned over to the workers, and the workers did just what might be expected: they first raised wages and then found they had to raise prices. Reliance on market competition eliminated some more inefficient producers, but in addition to the resulting inflation there was also waste and uneconomic investment that the backward Yugoslav society could ill afford.

By 1956, a drastic tightening of controls was necessary. Economic order was restored, but whereas earlier worker management was too uncontrolled, now it was too restricted. Necessary wage increases were held up, and in 1958 there were—to the shock of the leadership—a series of strikes by workers who in theory controlled their own enterprises. As a result, a new trend toward relaxation was decreed, and for a while it appeared that a proper balance was at hand. Production soared, and with two exceptionally good harvests, Yugoslavia began to experience an unprecedented boom.

Now, once again, with prosperity on the horizon, there was pressure for more liberalization. In 1961, virtually all wage restrictions were removed; and controls on prices, production and even foreign trade were greatly relaxed. To ease the impact of freer imports, $275 million in Western credits was negotiated. One of the aims of the new program was to boost the supply of consumer goods. This succeeded all too well. There was a veritable orgy of production, importation and buying of consumer goods—from electric stoves to automobiles. Prices soared, necessitated by sweeping wage increases and made possible by extensive, decentralized credit.

Production of basic industrial goods lagged, and so did exports —both vitally necessary to the precarious Yugoslav economy. With a foreign debt of nearly $800 million, the country ended the year with a hard currency adverse trade balance of $167 million. By the spring of 1962, the boom had turned into a capitalist-like crisis. Many enterprises were in serious trouble, and workers' councils began laying off employees. Tito, speaking from Diocletian's ancient city of Split, called a halt and ordered a return to tighter controls and more government direction.

The ups and downs of the economic system have a general although not absolute parallel in the political climate. The early decentralization was accompanied by the elimination of most of the harsher aspects of the police state and a wave of enthusiasm for a more democratic society. But here too—at least from the standpoint of the regime—things went too fast. By the end of 1953, Djilas was calling for the elimination of the Communist party altogether, with widespread popular approval both in and out of the party. Tito stepped in—somewhat reluctantly but firmly—to silence Djilas, or, more accurately, to try to silence him. For Djilas, with the courage and recklessness so typical of his native Montenegro, went on to demand two-party elections and finally—in *The New Class*—to oppose communism as a system in both its Yugoslav and Soviet guises.

Initially, Djilas was doing little more than spelling out what other members of the hierarchy—including Tito himself—had proclaimed as doctrine. It would be unfair and inaccurate to say that they were not sincere in talking, for instance, about a "withering away" of the party. But for them this was a theoretical position to be achieved only over the very long run and within a Communist framework—indeed as a means of implementing their peculiar brand of communism. For Djilas the system was not so important as democracy and he wanted to achieve it at once.

Tightening of Control

Although Djilas himself posed no threat to the regime's power, the impact of his ideas—widely publicized throughout Yugoslavia before his fall—was considerable and resulted in a serious disorientation, especially among younger members of the League of Communists, as the Yugoslav Communist party had been renamed in 1952. A tightening of party discipline was decreed, and there was a reassertion of party influence throughout the country. Criticism was discouraged. There was no return to the earlier police state, but there were political trials of minor figures. Ill-disguised intimidation of dissidents occurred, particularly in the more backward areas where many party bureaucrats had never really approved of the new system.

The new political freedom had been an indispensable factor in making economic decentralization and local autonomy meaningful; now party interference began to cut down on freedom of workers' councils and people's committees. This, too, led to abuses and produced widespread if muted grumbling. Public opinion in Yugoslavia does not determine policy, but can influence it; and especially when accompanied by such manifestations as strikes, public opinion could not be ignored. Worried by the extent of party interference, the League of Communists' top body, the Executive Committee, denounced abuses of party authority and privilege in 1958 in phrases resembling Milovan Djilas on the new class, albeit without Djilas' anti-Communist overtones. The ensuing freer political climate was marked by increased public discussion, a liberalized criminal code, an end to harassment of regime critics (like Vladimir Dedijer) and finally in 1961, the release of Djilas from prison.

The question in 1962 was whether the new economic controls would again be followed by a political crackdown with totalitarian overtones. The reimprisonment of Djilas, after publication abroad of his innocuous book, *Conversations with Stalin,* may have been occasioned more by personal pique on the part of Tito and the hierarchy than by politics, but it did not augur well. Neither did Tito's call for a resurgence of party discipline, his warnings against criticism of the regime and his attacks on "decadent phenomena" in art and literature. At the same time, by the end of the year there was no evidence of the kind of party and police intimidation which reappeared in 1956. On the contrary, a good deal of public discussion of the new proposed constitution was frank and spirited, and the constitution itself contained provisions that seemed intended not only to safeguard against any return to totalitarianism but also to further the trend away from it.

One question mark in all this, however, is the future of Yugoslavia's relations with the Soviet Union. In the past, regardless of cause and effect relationship, the trend toward tighter control in the economy and in politics coincided with moves toward rapprochement with the U.S.S.R.; and the reverse trend toward liberalization began when these efforts broke down. The current Yugoslav-Soviet rapprochement has gone further than ever before, and it remains to be seen what, if any, effect it will have on internal affairs.

In 1957, believing that he could influence the course of events in the Soviet Union and in the Communist world generally, Tito seemed ready to become a "nonmember" of the Soviet bloc of states. At that time Moscow's price for amity was too high. Soviet demands for changes in Yugoslav theory and practice and for acceptance of Moscow's leadership in foreign policy would have meant a virtual end to Yugoslav independence. At the last minute Tito, despite his strong desire for Communist solidarity, refused to go along, and the effort at rapprochement ended with bitter recriminations on both sides.

Today, however, the situation has changed. Tito is still unwilling to give up independence, but he feels certain that he is not being asked to. Moreover, he believes that he has succeeded in influencing Soviet policies. As seen from Belgrade, the comparative freedom achieved by the Soviet satellites reflects a genuine acceptance of the Yugoslav insistence of "independent paths to socialism.". . .

The role of the Chinese Communists is itself an important factor in bringing Yugoslavia and the Soviet Union together. Violent opponents of Titoism, the Chinese . . . also used Yugoslavia as a stalking horse in their quarrel with the U.S.S.R. in no small degree because they . . . [saw] Khrushchev becoming a Titoist, at least on broad questions of foreign policy. In addition, the Chinese have pried Albania loose from Soviet influence, and the Albanians have always been bitter and unreconstructed anti-Titoists. It is not unnatural that the greater the gulf between Moscow and Peking-Tirana, the narrower the gulf between Moscow and Belgrade.

Neutralist Policy

While the Belgrade view of all this may not be without merit, Yugoslavia's economic problems and Western policies—particularly American—also play a part. The fact is that Yugoslavia's independent neutralist position, so often jibing with Moscow's, was never well received in Washington. At his 1961 conference of neutralist nations in Belgrade, Tito reiterated earlier criticisms of the West at the same time refraining from criticizing the Soviet resumption of nuclear testing. Ambassador George Kennan [he resigned in 1963], who had been led to believe that Tito's performance would be more pleasing to the United States, took almost personal affront, and his reports to the State Department were partly responsible for the violent reaction of the Kennedy administration. This in turn contributed to congressional action restricting aid to Yugoslavia to agricultural shipments and denying Yugoslavia the most-favored-nation treatment extended to non-Soviet bloc countries. Both Ambassador Kennan and the Administration objected to this action, feeling it tended to push Yugoslavia further toward the Kremlin, without apparently recognizing their own responsibility for it.

Although congressional action wounded Yugoslavia pride, the Yugoslavs were somewhat philosophical about it, especially since the Administration was trying to have the discrimination removed. (Foreign Secretary Popovic told this writer last year that he realized the legislative restriction did not reflect Administration views. And he added: "Every country has its peculiar people. What distinguishes the United States is that you put them in your parliament.") The impact on the Yugoslav economy was more severe, at least potentially. Nearly 60 per cent of Yugoslav trade is now with the West, and the United States occupies first place in Yugoslav imports and third place in exports. Without aid, the decrease in exports, certain to result if tariff discrimination stands, would necessitate sharp reduction in important purchases from the United States. . . .

This development occurred at the same time Belgrade was worrying about trade exclusion from Western Europe as a result of Common Market policies. Although the Yugoslavs did not wish to join either the Common Market or the Soviet trading bloc, they feared exclusion from both. The Common Market countries showed less inclination than the Eastern bloc to permit a special trading relationship. As a result the Yugoslavs were particularly conscious of possible advantages of closer relations with the Soviet Union. At the same time, Tito realized that neither in trade nor aid can the East provide what Yugoslavia needs. If nothing else, this will undoubtedly move Belgrade to try to maintain friendly relations with the West. Whether they can or not is something else.

Yugoslavia almost certainly will not relinquish its independence, but Tito's yen for Communist solidarity plus Western refusal to accept this without reprisals, could, given economic difficulties, push Yugoslavia further into the Soviet bloc than anybody at present wants to go. Up until now, Belgrade's bargaining position with Moscow has been good. Without hope of aid or trade from the West, increasing economic troubles in Yugoslavia could put the U.S.S.R. in a much better position to make demands. Many in Yugoslavia as well as elsewhere fear that in such case the demands might be high.

This worries some Yugoslav Communists. If some of them support Tito's desire to become a "nonmember" of the bloc, others would like to emphasize the "non" instead of the "bloc." Here Tito's role as the prime mover for closer relations with the Soviet Union brings up the problem of Titoism after Tito.

The Yugoslav chieftain is seventy-one years old as of May 25, 1963. While neither his demise nor his retirement appear imminent, the question of his successor is perhaps the most absorbing, publicly undiscussed problem in Yugoslav politics. More than the extent of Yugoslavia's solidarity with the Soviet bloc is involved. On the one hand, many Yugoslav Communists, especially the younger ones, venerate Tito for his accomplishments. But they tend to regard him as a block to the kind of liberalizing direction they think Titoism should logically follow. On the other hand, Tito has qualities of leadership and personal magnetism not easily replaceable in a dictatorship that tries to base itself on popular approval of ethnic groups (whose past is one of bitter conflict).

The obvious choice for succession lies between the two vice presidents, Edvard Kardelj, a Slovene, and Aleksandar Rankovic, a Serb. Neither has the kind of "political it" Tito possesses, and the selection of either could well exacerbate ethnic feeling among the republics.

What is likely to happen, is that Kardelj and Rankovic together will succeed Tito, splitting functions as provided in an article of the new constitution [adopted in 1963] written to cope with just this problem. Under this arrangement Rankovic would take over formal direction of the League of Communists and become ceremonial head of the republic, while Kardelj, keeping a high party post, would take the reins of the government administration as president of the Federal Executive Council, a new post. Such a division reflects the work of the two men now, operating under Tito's general but increasingly inactive direction. While Rankovic is thought to place more emphasis on Communist solidarity than Kardelj, the difference between them thus far has been one of degree only. Actually, the main importance of succession will lie less in the new leadership than in the change itself, overdue after nearly eighteen years.

The new constitution . . . apparently recognizes the need for change, but only on levels below Tito. One provision limits the tenure of future presidents of the republic to two four-year terms and the tenure of members of parliament to one four-year term. Whether this latter limitation will affect Kardelj and Rankovic remains to be seen.

Despite the problems inherent in succession most observers feel that the regime has enough stability to surmount them and that the infighting for power of the Soviet variety is unlikely. At this juncture, to talk about the first succession in a regime like Yugoslavia's is like talking about the pudding before it is even baked, let alone eaten. The proof is yet to come.

YUGOSLAVIA REMAPS AGRICULTURE [15]

First of the major changes envisaged in Yugoslav economic methods is already under way in agriculture. It represents a government effort to induce Yugoslavia's peasants to produce more and enable them to sell as they please on a largely "free" market. It will mean better prices for farmers than the "guaranteed" ones offered by the state. Generally, these prices have been set too low in order to ensure inexpensive food for the townspeople. Thus they failed to induce the farmers to raise much more than they needed for themselves and local demands.

A next step is to be the reduction of taxes. The two moves together, it is said, will begin to put profit into Yugoslav farming

[15] From "Belgrade Remaps Agriculture," by Eric Bourne, special correspondent, *Christian Science Monitor.* p 3. S. 4, '64. Reprinted by permission from *The Christian Science Monitor.* © 1964 The Christian Science Publishing Society. All rights reserved.

and permit big cuts in the costly state subsidies it has required hitherto.

In theory, Yugoslavia's peasant farmers have been "free" for more than a decade. The Yugoslav Communists abandoned collectivization in 1953. Since then, their aim has been a "gradual" socialization of the countryside. The idea was to enlarge the remnants of land left as the so-called "Socialist sector"—the state farms and a few collectives—by persuading private peasants to "cooperate" with it or by buying land from them where they were willing to sell.

The regime devised a system of cooperation in which peasants could enter yearly contracts with a collective farm. The contracts obliged them—in return for fertilizer and machinery—to produce specific crops for sale to the state at guaranteed prices. The system was free. Peasants could decide themselves whether they made such contracts. But the percentage of Yugoslavia's current ten million private farmers who did so is very small.

The Yugoslav parliament was told recently that—after ten years of this attempt at "cooperation by persuasion"—of twelve million hectares (about 30 million acres) of arable land only slightly more than 10 per cent is "Socialist." Nonetheless this 10 per cent accounted for one third of all agricultural production and for almost two third of total deliveries. The explanation is that the private farmers have been producing principally for themselves. The state's prices were no spur to do otherwise. . . .

The proposal now is for a new system based on free price levels instead of the fixed or guaranteed prices.

A measure passed by parliament is to permit the private farmers to sell at "economic" prices regulated by supply and demand. The government will still be in the market to buy at its own guaranteed prices, which it has now already substantially increased. But the farmers will be free to offer their products on the open market first, said Vice President Edvard Kardelj, at "more favorable prices." In allowing prices to find their own level freely, the government will intervene only to protect the consumer by ensuring that these prices do not soar above certain limits.

Another leading Communist, Vladimir Bakaric, declared recently that the problems of private farming must be solved along lines favorable to farmers if agricultural output is to be lifted. He also condemned the "present old feudal-economic way" of trying to solve the problems by "orders from above."

A year ago, Soviet Premier Nikita S. Khrushchev commended some Yugoslav methods in economic management. Some of the Eastern Europeans have since begun to take a hard look at the Yugoslav way of doing things . . . [in view of its economic potential].

THE FUTURE OF EASTERN EUROPE [16]

How do present East-West relations affect the countries of Eastern Europe? What can they expect if there is a genuine relaxation of tension? Can they hope for more freedom, more independence, perhaps even a dissolution of the compulsory ties that now bind them to the Soviet Union? With these questions in mind, the author interviewed five experts on Soviet and East European affairs.

What direction will the current trend toward relaxation take in Eastern Europe?

PROFESSOR HENRY L. ROBERTS: I would think that basically there will be a positive development in Eastern Europe. Whether the changes will come as fast as one would hope for in every direction, I don't know. I think the process will involve a great deal of pulling and hauling, with ups and downs, but each in a quite different style. I suspect that what happens in Rumania, where there have been quite interesting developments in the last year or so, will have a quite different flavor from what occurs in

[16] From interview by George Mueller, a lawyer from Hungary, with Daniel Bell, professor of sociology, Columbia University; John C. Campbell, senior research fellow, Council on Foreign Relations; Louis Fischer, authority on Soviet affairs; Philip Mosely, director of the European Institute, Columbia University; and Henry L. Roberts, director of the Russian Institute, Columbia University. In *East Europe*. 13:11-15. My. '64. Reprinted by permission.

Czechoslovakia. Yugoslavia and Poland have been in the past somewhat special cases in the East European field. When one looks at each closely, the style of its departure from the Soviet norm is quite different. Although they've both had patterns of relaxation and then retreat, they seem to me to follow different impulses, which are undoubtedly connected with national styles of life, history, personality of leaders. On the whole, I would anticipate an amelioration of the general picture.

PROFESSOR PHILIP MOSELY: I think there will be a leveling up gradually. There will be setbacks and there will be new advances after a period of cautious recovery. But there are matters of national tradition and temperament that do enter into this. For example, there's no prospect that the Communist regime in East Germany can follow a process of relaxation. If it were to do so it would disappear. On the other hand, I think that we see in the attitude of the intelligentsia in Hungary and Poland a reflection of a very long association with, and contribution to, Western civilization which makes them reach out, often at great risk, to reassert the national tradition. . . .

PROFESSOR JOHN C. CAMPBELL: There's no question that there are different degrees of relative freedom or of mutual tolerance between the people and the regimes. And the contrast between Czechoslovakia and Hungary a year ago, for example, was very strong, very stark. Now certain changes have taken place in Czechoslovakia and maybe we can see a development in the direction Hungary has taken. That seems quite clear from some of the political statements that have been made and the purges of some of the prominent people in the Communist party of Czechoslovakia. This seems to be following the general trend and the Russians are not against it. As a matter of fact, they've done a great deal to stimulate this sort of thing because those who have held onto power beyond their period of usefulness, in Czechoslovakia for example, or Bulgaria, have been more or less Stalinist in outlook.

What maximum liberties could the countries of Eastern Europe expect if the current trends were to continue?

PROFESSOR MOSELY: It seems to me that the best prospect is to improve their economic relations with the outside world, to get a greater variety of resources, of equipment, of industrial and other ideas, and to avoid the dependence on the Soviet Union which has so often led to exploitation in their so-called commercial relations. Again, in the intellectual field these countries have very little to learn from the Soviet Union, except in the field of technology and science. And they have a great deal to give to the Soviet Union.

PROFESSOR DANIEL BELL: These [things], it seems to me, are quite variable. In Poland, for example, you have a tightening, in large part because the regime has had some economic difficulties and now has to mobilize its people and bring more pressures upon them. Since you're going to have to press the workers a bit, you do not want to allow the freer areas of criticism and you begin to crack down in other areas as well. In Czechoslovakia, conversely, the old Stalinist type of economic system has been running into difficulties. Therefore, you have to admit types of criticism in order to shake up that aspect of it. So you have a constant process of tightening or loosening in response to the crises which are endemic to this or any system. I think that the over-all point that is important is this: these are mobilized societies which have to keep moving and therefore you have to keep mobilizing the people. The pace of the mobilization, the degree of criticism, can tighten or expand in response to the particular economic situation you're in at the moment. But there is one very important change which is very crucial and which distinguishes the present from the Stalinist period. The Stalinist period was really what used to be called "The Age of the Lie." You cannot again lie so easily and this, it seems to me, is the most important, overriding difference between this period and the previous periods.

PROFESSOR CAMPBELL: It is difficult to say. Poland won certain liberties. Both the regime and the people insisted on them in 1956 and they were permitted by the Soviet Union. There has been a certain amount of retrogression in Poland in freedom of speech and freedom of expression in the arts, etc. Nevertheless, these freedoms, which grew out of the October crisis in 1956, have basically remained in force. I think it is true to say that the other East European countries have not arrived at this point. I don't see any reason in principle why they should not eventually do so. The real question is whether anyone can go beyond that, whether they can be allowed to have any kind of independent foreign policy—that's the real test. Yugoslavia does have such an independent foreign policy, because it really broke all the ties back in 1948-1949. So long as these other countries are in the Soviet camp, in the Soviet security system, in the economic system in which the Soviet Union is the leading factor, it is very difficult for them to go beyond a certain relaxation which gives them freedom in the arts and which allows some freedom of expansion or which gives them greater control over their economic policies than before. But there are limits.

What bearing has the German problem on the future of Eastern Europe?

PROFESSOR MOSELY: This is a very key problem because even if the people of Poland and Czechoslovakia, for example, could exercise real political self-determination, which the Soviets demand for people throughout Asia and elsewhere, they would still be very much afraid of a revived Germany. I feel that it is essential in the near future for the West to make it even clearer than it has that the Western boundaries of Czechoslovakia and Poland are going to remain. People have adjusted to these changes of population. I think that there are many people in West Germany who would be very glad to confirm the present boundaries with both Poland and Czechoslovakia if at the same time Germany could be reunited. Because the German people will also eventually have to have the right of self-determination. But we in the West are very anxious that this be carried out in a way that protects the vital interests of Czechoslovakia and Poland.

If the Soviet Union no longer had reason to fear a re-
militarized Germany, would she still want to retain her
"buffer" zone in the countries of Eastern Europe?

PROFESSOR ROBERTS: I would say yes. It seems to me that the
Soviet interest in Eastern Europe has always been more than just
strategic and certainly more than strategically defensive. Extension of its power to this area after the war was accompanied by
enormous social transformations, by the creation of Communist
regimes. It always seemed to go beyond the requirements of
military strategy and at the moment I feel the Soviet Union
would be very reluctant to see any state lose the "benefits" of this
dispensation. I think this in itself would be a very serious loss
and would be in a sense quite independent of the military
picture.

PROFESSOR MOSELY: This would require a basic change of
Soviet and Communist objectives. They would have to decide
that the present division of Europe should be softened, that there
should be greater expansion of internal self-determination in
many fields within the countries of East Central Europe and they
would have to be satisfied with having only strategic preponderance in the area. This would be going back to what the United
States in effect agreed to at Yalta. We did not agree that they
had the right to communize any of these parts. We tried to protect
the right of each people to have its own self-determination. But
we recognized, because of the war and the great power of the
Soviet Union, that it would have a preponderant strategic influence in the area. It was, perhaps, just not feasible to persuade
them to stop short of communizing the area. At the end of World
War II, I was a strong advocate of keeping Germany demilitarized
but united. Under the occupation this would have meant carrying
out the Potsdam Agreement for free elections at different levels,
of assuring freedom of association of parties, of information, of the
press and religion. I helped to draft the treaty that the United
States proposed in April of 1946, a twenty-five-year treaty to hold
Germany demilitarized but to treat it as a single political unit,
except for the concessions of territory that would have to be made

to Poland. And I was very disappointed that we couldn't work it out along this line. It seems to me that we could certainly return to this if the Soviet Union would make clear that it is no longer trying to get a hold on Germany and with it the whole of Western Europe. And that we could agree not on a completely demilitarized Germany but on one which had the size and quality of its armaments regulated under inspection. I feel that the Soviet leadership was not at all sincere in expressing a fear of German rearmament when it begun to occur and that if they had wanted to really bring about a relaxation of tension permanently in Europe, they could have allowed Germany to be reunited under strategic controls against rearmament, but with some forces to protect their own borders. That would mean they would be able to relax the pressure on East Central Europe.

What would be the United States' attitude toward a bilateral treaty by which Soviet troops would be withdrawn from Eastern Europe in return for a settlement of the German question satisfactory to the Soviet Union?

PROFESSOR ROBERTS: Well, I think the United States would certainly be pleased if the troops of the Soviet Union were within the Soviet Union. I'm certain that we would welcome some resolution of the German difficulties so, as you put it, I don't see the problem from our side. The problem would be to find an arrangement that would be acceptable to the Soviet Union's notion of its interest. It would be very difficult indeed. I've wrestled off and on with this particular problem of finding formulae for linking these two parts over a number of years and they are very hard to come by. I'm not particularly anxious to say when both sides could see eye to eye on any formula for this.

PROFESSOR MOSELY: This raises very tempting and also very complicated possibilities. Now, one problem is that, in my opinion, the East German Communist regime would not survive without Soviet troops in its own territory. This at once raises the question whether the Soviet Union can afford such an undertaking as withdrawal of its troops from East Germany. In the case of Poland there are relatively small numbers of troops and I don't know just how many there are in Hungary now.

I think we would have to have an agreement on the reunification of Germany in order to carry this out. And the Soviet Union is not interested in this of course, [but] if we could bring about the reunification of the German people in their present boundaries in peace, and a reconciliation between the Germans and the peoples of East Central Europe, I think we would. This is only my guess. But it seems to me that this would be such a major improvement in the security of the peoples of Poland, Czechoslovakia, Hungary, as well as of Western Europe, that we would give it every consideration.

How do you see the political future of Eastern Europe if present trends continue?

PROFESSOR ROBERTS: Well, its political future in a way would be without precedent if relaxation continued to a point where it became independent of the Soviet Union. It seems to me that the central fact of the historical past of Eastern Europe is a series of unsatisfactory situations. Precarious independence in the interwar period existed under a constant threat from outside and before that there was a period of domination. So one would hope that in the future we will really have some new political structuring of this area. There has been some rather interesting thought I've encountered among some writers in recent years concerning federal structures involving connections with the movement toward a type of unity with Western Europe. Now this would seem to me, of course, the ultimately ideal solution, but this is a very hard thing indeed to bring about.

PROFESSOR CAMPBELL: Well, I think if you had what would amount to a rather radical change in Soviet policy, they could establish more natural ties both among themselves and with Western Europe. This would not mean coming directly into organizations like the Common Market; nevertheless, strong ties could be knit between Western and Eastern Europe so that, for Americans particularly, I think we should realize that the "East

European problem," as we've been inclined to call it, is not just a separate problem, is not just a factor in the relation between the United States and the Soviet Union but that these countries are part of Europe. That this is their tradition, and we would hope in the long run that this would be their future.

———

The specialists all seemed to feel that the trend toward liberalization in Eastern Europe is a continuing one, possibly irreversible, although likely to be accompanied by retreats and retrogressions. Recent developments—particularly in Czechoslovakia, Hungary and Rumania—were seen as evidence that the process will follow different paths in different countries. The fact that the Soviet Union has taken no visible steps to restrict these developments seems to indicate that the Soviet leaders are prepared to accept them. However, there is a range of opinion as to how far the liberalization process will actually be permitted to go. Professor Campbell, for example, feels that as long as the East European countries are in the Soviet orbit, their independence cannot exceed the limits which the Soviet Union considers to be in its own interest.

The conclusion seems to be that the satellite countries have become more than just a military buffer zone for the Soviet Union. They are such an integral part of the postwar Soviet empire that true independence is impossible without a much more fundamental reorganization than now seems likely. A more optimistic view was presented by Louis Fischer, the well-known journalist and author now teaching at Princeton University. His response to a question along these lines was:

> The Soviet Union can maintain friendly relations with the countries of Eastern Europe without dominating them, just as there's more business being done by England in India today—in free India—than when India was a colony. There's no reason at all why Czechoslovakia should not be on friendly political terms with the Soviet Union and be free. The same is true of Poland and Hungary and all the others. I think some day in Moscow there will come a realization that it is not necessary to rule a colony in order to benefit economically. There's greater benefit without colonization.

There was general agreement that expansion of contacts—economic and cultural—with the West would contribute to liberalization. The long-term possibilities were outlined by Professor Mosely in the following terms:

I would hope that in many modest ways the people of East Central Europe would be able to expand pursuit of their own interests. I think this would mean redefining their own purposes. Because of the strategic situation, it would mean accepting the preponderance of Communist power, but trying to give it a different content. In Polish history there was a period called the period of "small deeds." It was a period of realism in which Polish industry and science and culture made great strides despite the absence of political freedom and national freedom. Perhaps for the next ten years or so all of the peoples of Eastern Europe, except the East Germans who are in an impossible position, are going to have an opportunity to redefine the content of their system of rule to an extent that will give them greater satisfaction, greater continuity with their own national traditions and a greater participation in both the technological and intellectual development of the entire world, and particularly that of the West.

IV. THE UNITED STATES AND EASTERN EUROPE

EDITOR'S INTRODUCTION

U.S. policies toward Eastern Europe in the past twenty years have generated an unusual amount of debate and bitterness. Criticism of U.S. action or inaction—as the case may be—began when the Soviet Army swept into the area during World War II. The criticism continued during the early postwar years when the Soviet Union violated the letter and the intent of Allied wartime agreements. In 1956, many believed that the United States and the West betrayed the Hungarians by not helping them in their rebellion against their Communist masters and the Soviet Union. Today, the attack on U.S. policies toward Eastern Europe is led by those who think that in our efforts to relax world tensions we are likely to grant much but receive little. The critics refer, for instance, to our willingness to trade with the Communist countries in the hope that such contacts may further improve relations between East and West.

This section offers a range of articles on U.S. policies toward Eastern Europe and includes some representative criticisms of those policies. The first piece reviews the course of U.S. policy toward Eastern Europe since the end of the war. It discusses, among other things, the pros and cons of "containment" and "liberation." This is followed by a congressional study setting out general guidelines and considerations for U.S. policy toward Eastern Europe. Although the study appeared in 1960, many of its observations remain pertinent today. President Johnson's 1964 "bridge building" speech, which currently sets the tone for U.S. policies, is briefly quoted. It is followed by an article analyzing the implications of the speech. George F. Kennan then discusses some of the considerations involved in East-West trade. The section concludes with a speech by U.S. Ambassador to West

Germany George McGhee reviewing the entire Eastern European scene and outlining some of our broad policy aims in that area.

As several of these selections note, however, it should not be forgotten that there are limits to what the United States and the West can do. Eastern Europe is plainly within the Soviet sphere of influence and it is hardly to be imagined that the Kremlin will allow the region to slip away. Changes yes, diversity yes, more liberalization perhaps—but, for the present, only up to a point.

BREACHING THE BARRIERS [1]

The Communist seizure of control of Eastern Europe after World War II aroused deep concern in the U.S. and stimulated widespread controversy. Could a different U.S. strategy during the war have kept all or part of the region out of Communist hands?

Would the threat or use of force by the Western allies have compelled Moscow to implement wartime agreements providing for free elections and self-government in Eastern Europe after World War II? At a time when the U.S. was demobilizing rapidly, when public sentiment in the West strongly favored the preservation of Big Five Unity, and an exhausted world wished to turn to peacetime reconstruction, was such a policy possible?

Containment and Liberation

By early 1948 the Communists had completed their take-over of Eastern Europe. Western Europe, still trying to recover from the war, seemed dangerously exposed to Soviet pressures. To meet the threat, the U.S. adopted wide-ranging and unprecedented countermeasures. Under the Truman Doctrine, the U.S. had already extended aid to Greece and Turkey. Under the Marshall Plan, it helped Western Europe recover from the devastation of war and regain political and social stability. NATO raised a U.S. military umbrella over our European allies and protected them from the danger of aggression.

[1] From *Great Decisions 1965*. (Fact Sheet no. 5. Eastern Europe—End of the Satellite Era?) Foreign Policy Association. 345 E. 46th St. New York, N.Y. 10017. '65. p 56-8. Copyright 1965 by the Foreign Policy Association, Inc. Reprinted by permission.

These preventive and restorative measures came to be associated with a policy approach known as "containment." The man credited with first using the term in this context was George F. Kennan, then head of the State Department's Policy Planning Staff. "The main element of any U.S. policy toward the Soviet Union," wrote Kennan in 1947, "must be that of a long-term, patient but firm and vigilant containment of Russian expansive tendencies. . . . Soviet pressure against the free institutions of the Western world is something that can be contained by the adroit and vigilant application of counterforce at a series of constantly shifting geographical and political points, corresponding to the shifts . . . of Soviet policy. . . ."

By the end of the Truman Administration—despite the fact that Western Europe was on the road to recovery and the direct Soviet threat to the area was receding—the policy of containment was being subjected to increasing attack. Critics charged that it was a defensive policy which put the U.S. in the position of responding to Soviet moves and left the cold war initiative in Moscow's hands. As for Eastern Europe, critics contended that containment accepted Soviet control of the area as part of the status quo and thus, in effect, permanently wrote off the people of Eastern Europe to the Communists.

In the 1952 presidential campaign, debate over U.S. policy toward Eastern Europe played a prominent role. The 1952 platform of the victorious Republicans promised an alternative to containment—liberation. A policy of liberation, the platform stated, "will mark the end of the negative, futile and immoral policy of 'containment'. . . . The policies, we espouse will inevitably set up strains and stresses within the captive world which will make the rulers impotent to continue their monstrous ways and mark the beginning of their end."

As many Republicans saw it, liberation meant that, at the least, the United States would go over to the cold war offensive and pursue vigorous economic, political and propaganda policies that would create turmoil within Eastern Europe and eventually force Moscow to relinquish its grip.

Did liberation ever promise more than this? Many both in this country and abroad believed it did. They believed it committed the United States to a policy of active intervention to secure freedom for Eastern Europeans when and if the right moment came along.

Such a moment seemed to have come when the East Berliners revolted in 1953. Soviet troops crushed the uprising. The United States did not intervene.

An even more favorable moment occurred when revolution swept Hungary in 1956. For a brief few days the revolutionaries held power and moved to quit the Soviet bloc. Soviet troops and tanks which had been withdrawn from Budapest returned to put down the revolt. The Hungarian government appealed to the outside world for aid. Again the United States did not intervene.

The lessons of these events were clear. The Soviet Union was willing to use force to maintain its position in Eastern Europe; the United States was not willing to use force to change the status quo.

The events in Hungary engendered considerable bitterness among many here and in Eastern Europe. They felt that the United States propaganda agencies had given Eastern Europeans reason to believe this country would not stand passively by if they rebelled against their Communist rulers. The State Department attempted to clarify its position on liberation beyond any possible misunderstanding. "We do not incite violent revolt," U.S. Secretary of State John Foster Dulles said in 1957; "rather we encourage an evolution to freedom. . . . And when some steps are made toward independence, we show a readiness to respond with friendly acts."

But did liberation so construed differ radically from containment? The Truman Administration had responded with "friendly acts" by sending military and economic aid to Yugoslavia after Marshal Tito's break with Stalin. President Eisenhower had continued that policy. After 1956, as Poland showed signs of independence from Moscow, the United States began shipping it surplus agricultural goods and granted credits for the purchase of American agricultural machinery.

Bridges or Pressure

Under the administrations of Presidents Kennedy and Johnson, the United States has intensified efforts to encourage the regimes in power to move toward greater independence and internal diversity. It has made and welcomed overtures for friendlier relations with countries in the area. In 1961 the United States and Poland signed new trade agreements. In 1964 the United States and Rumania signed an economic agreement. Cultural exchange programs begun under President Eisenhower have been continued. Diplomatic relations with Hungary, Rumania and Bulgaria have been improved. "We must bring the countries of Eastern Europe closer to the Western community," said President Johnson in 1964. "We will continue to build bridges across the gulf which has divided us. . . ." [See "Building Bridges," in this section, below.]

Just as containment was attacked by advocates of liberation, current Administration policies are opposed by advocates of a "hard line." In 1963 the House of Representatives voted to amend the foreign-aid bill by banning the use of Government credits to help finance sales to Communist countries. Only intense Administration pressure brought the House to reverse its stand. In the 1964 Food for Peace act, despite Administration opposition, Congress prohibited Communist countries from paying for surplus foods in their own currencies. It required payment in dollars. Another provision banned long-term credits to countries dominated by the Soviet Union.

Hardliners, generally speaking, see little point in trying to distinguish between different varieties of communism and strongly oppose any accommodation with existing regimes in Eastern Europe. The policy of differentiating between "good" (Kadar, Tito, Gomulka) and "bad" (Chinese, Albanian) Communists, Senator Goldwater said during the [1964] presidential campaign, "has been an utter failure. It has failed to halt the march of communism. . . . This policy, if I may call it that, has instead helped the Communist world through a time of troubles and allowed it to emerge as a greater threat than ever to the freedom of the West." *Détente* diplomacy, hardliners maintain, tends to blind the free world to the irreconcilable hostility of communism, while trade and aid help the Communist rulers solve their internal difficulties and strengthen their hold on their captive peoples. The need, they insist, is for tougher policies. As the conservative publication, *National Review,* puts it, "we should mount and maintain pressures of all types, on and within the Communist empire, so as to induce new weaknesses and aggravate old ones. . . ."

Current Administration efforts to promote better relations with Eastern Europe are complicated by a number of problems involving West Germany. For example, German participation in the United States-sponsored multilateral fleet is bitterly opposed by every Communist government in Eastern Europe. On this issue, the Communist regimes are able to rally popular support from people who have suffered from German aggression in the past and who apparently still fear a revival of German militarism.

Poland has another cause for concern. At the end of World War II the Soviet Union incorporated into its territory the eastern part of Poland, which Poland had taken from the Soviet Union in 1920. As compensation Poland was allowed to occupy former German lands to the west. This territory, from which some 10 million Germans were deported back to Germany and in which 7 million Poles now live, extends to the Oder-Neisse rivers, the current border of East Germany.

The Soviet Union officially recognizes the Oder-Neisse line as final and permanent. The United States does not, holding that the present border does not have legal international status until a German peace treaty is signed. Thus Moscow is able to claim it is the guarantor and protector of the territorial integrity of Poland.

Some experts who endorse the Administration's bridge-building policies toward Eastern Europe believe that Washington must be more responsive than it has been to the legitimate Eastern European fears of West Germany. They urge that the United States recognize the Oder-Neisse line and that it reconsider and abandon sponsorship of a multilateral nuclear fleet in which

Germany would participate. They suggest, too, that the United States turn a more receptive ear to Eastern European proposals for a nuclear-free zone in Central Europe (including part of West Germany), and for some form of military disengagement in the area.

The Administration is aware that its position on the Oder-Neisse boundary, to which all administrations since 1945 have adhered, gives the Polish regime a popular issue to exploit. However, Washington feels it cannot officially recognize the Oder-Neisse without injuring its relations with West Germany, unless a German peace treaty is signed. But it has repeatedly indicated that it has no intention of upsetting the territorial arrangements that have given Poland former German territory. As for the inclusion of West Germany in a multilateral nuclear fleet, Washington contends that this is the best way of preventing that country from ever having its own independent nuclear arsenal. Finally, Washington maintains that it is always ready to consider plans for military disengagement in Central Europe, but that thus far Communist proposals have been unacceptable because they are aimed at upsetting the present balance of military power in Europe to the benefit of Moscow. . . .

For its part, the U.S. intends to continue its present approach of bridge building. Just a few days after Khrushchev's abrupt fall from power, President Johnson declared that the change "will not stop the forces in Eastern Europe that are working for greater independence. These forces will continue to have our sympathy. We will not give up our hope of building new bridges to these people."

The Administration remains convinced that bridge building benefits the free world by encouraging diversity and independence within Eastern Europe. It feels that tough policies will lead the regimes in power to become more repressive and to move closer to the Soviet Union for protection. All our Western allies more or less subscribe to this appraisal.

The hardliners reject this approach. They believe that nothing we can do will alter the fact that the Communist regimes of Eastern Europe are bound by ties of interest and ideology to

Moscow and that current U.S. policy permits them to strengthen their own positions. Only unrelenting pressure, in this view, can loosen the Communist grip on the area.

THE LIMITS OF POLICY [2]

For all the prolonged domestic controversy in the United States over the Yalta and other wartime agreements and over "containment versus liberation," the nature of our relations with the peoples of Eastern Europe remains confused, and much of the debate has seemed to lack real content. To some extent this is because the terms of the problem have changed with the passage of time. In the months surrounding the end of the Second World War there was a real conflict between those who would accept Communist rule in Eastern Europe, either as a "progressive" advance or as a necessary and supportable price for continued "Big Three" cooperation, and those who felt that American military forces, then still in Europe, should, if necessary, be used to make the Soviet Union observe its commitments and to prevent the westward expansion of communism. But the grounds supporting both sides of this dispute disappeared in the period that followed: few Americans were still able to find any virtues in Communist rule, the wartime alliance quickly dissolved, the great American armies came home, and within a few years the Soviet Union came to be a power enjoying an abundance of both thermonuclear and conventional armaments.

Under these new circumstances the necessary concern with shoring up the defenses of Western Europe soon came to have, and continues to have, a higher priority than trying to alter the situation in Eastern Europe. Despite the fact that the threat to Western Europe stemmed in part from the Soviet advance into Eastern Europe, improved defense through NATO rather than counterattack against the Soviet salient seemed the only feasible military response. As for nonmilitary efforts to bring about an

[2] From *U.S.S.R. and Eastern Europe;* a study of U.S. foreign policy, prepared at the request of the Committee on Foreign Relations, United States Senate, by a Columbia-Harvard research group. United States. Senate. 86th Congress, 2d session. Supt. of Docs. Washington, D.C. 20402. '60. no 11. p 70-3.

improved measure of sovereignty, self-determination, and freedom for the peoples of Eastern Europe, attempts through diplomacy were frustrated by the simple fact that the Soviet Union showed no inclination to relinquish Communist control over any of the "peoples' democracies." Any diplomatic bargains on this point promised only to weaken the West, chiefly through Germany, without assuring a real retraction of Communist power. As for the hopes that domestic resistance and opposition might lead to a retraction or extensive modification of Communist rules, these were first raised and then dashed by the events of 1956 in Poland and Hungary. While these events demonstrated that an externally imposed totalitarian regime could be dislodged, under certain circumstances, by domestic opposition, they also demonstrated that the Soviet Union was ready, and able, to put down such threats to its orbit and that effective American support of popular uprisings would carry serious risk of setting off a general war.

Since 1956 the United States has been confronted by the fact that, although Eastern Europe now enjoys more variety and relative relaxation than in the Stalin era, it remains an area of great importance and sensitivity to the Soviet Union, which has made it perfectly clear that it will forcefully oppose any threats of "liberation" or detachment.

This being so, what policies are open to the United States for the future? Rather than review current debate, much of which seems anachronistic or is reduced to symbolic issues which show little promise of substantially influencing the course of events, it may be more fruitful to discuss certain considerations that should bear on U.S. policy toward Eastern Europe.

(1) U.S. policy should not work to provoke or exacerbate crises within Eastern Europe between the people and their Communist rulers. The slogan "the worse—the better," which the Communists have used on occasion, should not be ours. Not only would an explosion in Eastern Europe carry, as it did in 1956, serious danger of war, but this whole approach could only mean greater hardship for the peoples of the area. This is not to say that we can prevent explosions from occurring; they may be inherent in the situation the Communists themselves have created,

but it seems highly unlikely, to judge from recent experience, that the United States or the free world would benefit from a revolution which brought about Soviet reprisals and suppression; nor would such a convulsion be likely seriously to weaken the U.S.S.R. in the absence of a mortal crisis within the Soviet Union itself.

(2) The center of gravity of American foreign policy lies outside Eastern Europe, in the non-Communist world. It is there that we must build the strength to resist Communist pressures, in whatever form they may assume, and it is there that our policies have most chance of being effective. It is not a matter of exclusive alternatives but rather one of priorities in such things as the allocation of funds, diplomatic activity and attention. Unfortunately, we cannot save freedom through Eastern Europe; we can easily lose it through inattention elsewhere.

(3) A third consideration, much more difficult to resolve, arises from the fact that Eastern Europe is such a neuralgic point for the Soviet Union. It is an area in which the Soviet leaders have a major material and prestige stake, and which they are reluctant to negotiate about or even to discuss seriously. The Hungarian revolution in particular is a very touchy subject that produces only embarrassment, evasion, or anger on the part of Soviet spokesmen. But what follows from this? Should one avoid or soft-pedal this topic because it is so sensitive and may drive the Soviet leaders to vigilance and repression? Or should one press on this obviously vulnerable spot in the Soviet record and make the most of it? . . .

(4) The United States, whatever our expectations about an improvement or stabilization of Soviet-American relations and whatever the chances of stimulating Communist vigilance and repression, cannot for these reasons disregard the political and ethical grounds underlying our antipathy to what has happened to Eastern Europe since the war. While this antipathy is in some part a product of strategic considerations and in greater part a revulsion against cruelty and perfidy, it stems chiefly from a crass violation by the Soviet Union of the principle of self-determination—not necessarily national or ethnic self-determination (it may be that the peoples of Eastern Europe would have moved

toward some type of federation). While this principle encounters serious problems in application, both domestically and in international relations, it is doubtful whether the United States, as a democratic society, could abandon it without disarming itself at a most vital point. For is this not at the core of our conflict with communism: the latter's denial of "spontaneity" and its insistence that all decision and wisdom, all keys to the future reside in a self-appointed and self-perpetuating vanguard? We need not parade this principle and we must recognize its ambiguities (as in our own Civil War), but the striving for autonomy of decision is indispensable to any hope for a free society.

(5) Related to this consideration is a very practical, and largely defensive, reason why the United States cannot ignore the status of the nations in Eastern Europe: many features of Western policy to which the U.S.S.R. has made strenuous objections, such as NATO, our German policy, or our overseas bases, are in effect responses to the westward expansion of Communist power into Eastern Europe after the war. Inasmuch as it appears to be a central purpose of Soviet policy to force an abandonment of these policies, it is important—if only for purposes of international debate—not to let the underlying causes for these measures be lost from view. Otherwise we would be obliged to argue on the Soviet Union's terms: that NATO and other mutual defense efforts are gratuitous and aggressive measures for which there is no justification. Similarly, with respect to the Soviet charges of Western imperialism and colonialism, the examples of Communist exploitation and disregard of national independence in Eastern Europe are an important and indispensable point of rebuttal, not least for the Asian audience. . . .

(6) But if these considerations suggest that Eastern Europe cannot, and should not, be dropped as an area of concern for American foreign policy, they do not tell us how that concern should be expressed. In actual practice this must be a matter of common sense and discrimination. It is probably true that the Soviet Union would prefer the United States to renounce any interest in, or responsibility for, the shape of events in Eastern Europe, but it is also true that while certain actions or efforts

will only cause counteractions, others may have ameliorative effects. For example, talk about "liberation," which, however we may try to take the edge off the term by modifying its definition, carries overtones of forcibly wrenching Eastern Europe from the Soviet grasp, will only sharpen the Soviet response—and will sound dreadfully hollow to the East Europeans. On the other hand, accurate reporting about the state of affairs in Eastern Europe, an indication that the world knows what is going on, may check certain excesses. Indeed, on occasion skillfully handled diplomatic protests about certain abuses have brought useful results. But obviously such actions require an acute political sense of the art of the possible. Direct challenges on issues concerning which the Soviet regime feels that it has more to lose than to gain by some relaxation will only lead to a tightening of the reins. Whether these marginal alleviations that we can promote will prove to be cumulatively significant with the passage of time is impossible to say. But they are worth attempting for their own sakes.

(7) The role of contacts and exchanges—cultural, educational, commercial, and technical—may also be regarded as one of marginal alleviation which may have significant, if unmeasurable, results in the long run. It is obvious that the Communist regimes are of two minds about such activities: on the one hand, certain definite gains in information, techniques, and prestige; on the other, the danger of disturbing influences. The balance of these considerations evidently varies from country to country, including the Soviet Union. It is necessary for the United States to be prudent both in not pressing for more than the traffic can bear and also in not succumbing to the happy belief that exchanges can somehow dissolve the political and moral differences dividing us and the Soviet bloc. Whether we like it or not exchanges are part of the political encounter, which does not mean that we must regard all such activities as devices for propaganda and pressure; on the contrary, they are likely to be most effective if we, for our part at least, refrain from using them manipulatively. An educational exchange that serves the purposes of serious scholarship is more likely to be politically effective than

one which tries to use scholarship as a gimmick in psychological warfare.

It is difficult to measure the effects of exchanges and hence hard to estimate the effort and expense that should go to support them. At the present time, however, given the present combination of the "peaceful coexistence" line and the absence of many diplomatically negotiable issues in Eastern Europe, exchanges may constitute one of the most active fields of engagement and contact and for that reason are of considerable importance to public policy, even though much of the activity may be conducted through private American channels.

(8) With regard to the extent of differentiation that may develop among the states of Eastern Europe and the degree of permissible departure from the Soviet model, it is certainly in the American interest that the flat conformity of the Stalin era be replaced by a greater degree of expression of local interests and needs, even if the regimes are Communist. Even the reverse movement of the Gomulka government in recent months does not wholly cancel out the gains of the Polish October [of 1956].

But if variety and increased local decision in the Soviet orbit are to be welcomed, it would be unwise to regard growing diversity as the prelude to a disintegration of Communist power in Eastern Europe. Actually, some increased diversity, if kept within limits, might even act to stabilize the bloc in reducing the pressures that build up in enforcing rigid conformity.

Given the real limitations to American influence in Eastern Europe, it is doubtful whether U.S. policy can directly promote such autonomous developments. We are not in a position to break down doors, and the attitude of "rewarding" states by the degree to which they succeed in departing from the Soviet norm can easily serve to reinforce the image of American policy the Soviet Union wishes to create. On the other hand, the very variety, pluralism, and spontaneity of American society are such that its contacts with the states of Eastern Europe are almost inevitably productive of change and diversity. We should neither single out one or another Eastern Europe state as the object for our active attention (though some states are much more closed than others), nor should we disregard Eastern Europe and concern ourselves only with the Soviet Union. Rather we should be prepared, both in Eastern Europe and the Soviet Union, to foster such contacts with the people as can be made and to remove those barriers that can be removed. This is a limited goal but an important one and one that we can be perfectly frank about in discussions with the Communist leaders.

BUILDING BRIDGES [3]

There is no longer a single Iron Curtain. There are many. Each differs in strength and thickness, in the light that can pass through it and the hopes that can prosper behind it.

We do not know when all European nations will become part of a single civilization, but as President Eisenhower said in 1953, and I quote: "This we do know: A world that begins to witness the rebirth of trust among nations can find its way to peace that is neither partial nor punitive."

We will continue to build bridges across the gulf which has divided us from Eastern Europe. They will be bridges of increased trade, of ideas, of visitors and of humanitarian aid.

We do this for four reasons:

First, to open new relationships to countries seeking increased independence yet unable to risk isolation.

Second, to open the minds of a new generation to the values and the vision of the Western civilization from which they come and to which they belong.

Third, to give freer play to the powerful forces of legitimate national pride—the strongest barrier to the ambition of any country to dominate another.

Fourth, to demonstrate that identity of interest and the prospects of progress for Eastern Europe lie in a wider relationship with the West.

We go forward within the framework of our unalterable commitment to the defense of Europe and to the reunification

[3] From address delivered by President Lyndon B. Johnson, at the dedication of the George C. Marshall Research Library at Virginia Military Institute, Lexington, Virginia, May 23, 1964. Text from New York *Times.* p 46. My. 24, '64.

of Germany. But under the leadership of President Truman and President Eisenhower and our late beloved President Kennedy, America and Western Europe have achieved the strength and self-confidence to follow a course based on hope rather than hostility, based on opportunity rather than fear.

And it is also our belief that wise and skillful development of relationships with the nations of Eastern Europe can speed the day when Germany will be reunited.

We are pledged to use every peaceful means to work with friends and allies so that all of Europe may be joined in a shared society of freedom.

PUTTING EUROPE TOGETHER AGAIN [4]

Two new ideas about Eastern Europe seem to have come together in Mr. Johnson's thinking. A good deal turns on the way both of them are developed in the coming months. The first is the realization that, because there is no longer such a single thing as a "Communist bloc," there is room for a range of different Western policies towards the different Communist governments. This realization is not brand new. . . . But it has been left to Mr. Johnson, characteristically, to draw out the political implications. The aims of the new approach to Eastern Europe, said the President, included the desire "to open new relationships to countries seeking increased independence" and the hope of giving freer play to the "powerful forces of legitimate national pride."

The difficulty is that this could mean either one of two quite different things. If all Mr. Johnson wants to do is to take advantage of the fact that the Iron Curtain is more permeable to Western ideas at some places than at others, in the hope that the process will sooner or later become general, no more need be said, except good luck to him. The aim would then be a continuation of Mr. Kennedy's hope of eventually bringing the whole of the Russian-led alliance into a new and stabler relationship with the Western world. . . .

[4] From "Johnson over Elbe." *The Economist.* 211:924-6. My. 30, '64. Reprinted by permission.

But some of Mr. Johnson's phrases suggest a different interpretation. There are people who will see in the talk of "national pride" an attempt to exploit Eastern Europe's renascent nationalism in anti-Russian directions. In that case the objective would be not a change in the cold war relationship, but merely the expedient use of new opportunities for old cold war purposes; in a word, rollback, in a new guise.

If this were really what Mr. Johnson was driving at, it would be necessary to say that he might be going in a very wrong direction. For one thing, there would be a real danger of getting the political cart before the humanitarian horse, and running over the horse into the bargain. The main test of Western policy towards Eastern Europe (once the security of the West itself has been properly and firmly secured) is whether the policy helps to bring about an improvement in the life of the people who live there. . . .

What is more, there are severe limits to what can be achieved by a policy of promoting East European nationalism for anti-Russian ends. The hope of a lasting settlement between Moscow and the West—the "permanent peace" Mr. Johnson spoke of . . . still turns, as it always has turned, on working out a solution of the German problem acceptable on both sides of the dividing line. If the pot of nationalism in Eastern Europe bubbles up to a point where the Communist regime in East Germany looks like going pop, the Russians will certainly screw down the lid. And two can play the dividing game. Is it possible for the United States to encourage separatism in the eastern half of Europe without encouraging the same sort of divisive nationalism in the western half—a nationalism that the Russians can exploit in France today, maybe in Germany tomorrow?

Happily, the odds are that Mr. Johnson is thinking along more constructive lines than this. He doubtless finds it convenient not to spell things out too precisely: the idea of a new approach to Communist Europe will be swallowed more easily in Congress if it has a faint flavor of "liberation;" it probably does no harm to remind . . . [the Russians that their] part of Europe is not so tightly screwed together that it cannot be made to rattle a bit.

But it was suggested earlier in this article that here seemed to be two ideas behind Mr. Johnson's speech. The first—that there are advantages in treating different Communist countries differently— is probably less important than the second. This second idea is that for policy-making purposes the word "Europe" has lately changed its meaning.

This is the theme Mr. Walter Lippmann has recently been spelling out. . . . For all practical purposes, Mr. Lippmann observes, "Europe" has for the last eighteen years meant to most Western policy makers the non-Communist tail of the continent. It was this definition of Europe that shaped the decision of the early 1950's to make Germany safe against Russia by binding it militarily to the West, and shaped the attempt that is still going on to create a new political organization in Western Europe; the problem of what Western Europe's relations were to be with its Eastern neighbors was left to be settled later.

But in the last year or two, partly because both parts of the continent have rewon some of their lost self-confidence, Europe has begun to reassume its old, and real, meaning. The feeling that it is no longer possible to frame a policy based on the idea of two separate watertight European compartments has begun to have practical consequences on both sides of the Elbe. It is this growing search for ways of linking the two compartments that gives body to what might otherwise have been an empty phrase of Mr. Johnson's—the "bold design" of a community reconstructed "within its historic boundaries."

EAST-WEST TRADE [5]

When it comes to the trade of the United States with the [Communist] bloc, it seems to me that the first thing we could usefully do would be to relax and not to make such heavy sledding of it. In economic terms, this trade is still of minor importance. In the case of the Soviet Union, it amounted in 1961

[5] From *On Dealing with the Communist World*, by George F. Kennan, former U.S. Ambassador to the Soviet Union and Yugoslavia. Harper & Row (published for the Council on Foreign Relations). New York. '64. p 33-6. Copyright © 1964 by the Council on Foreign Relations, Inc. Reprinted by permission.

to only 1 per cent of the total Soviet trade, and something like two tenths of a per cent of ours. Communist countries are not going to be decisively benefited if this trade increases somewhat; nor are they going to be importantly injured if we restrict it still further. The Soviet government is not going to fall if we deny it wheat; and the heavens are not going to fall if we permit wheat to be shipped. The amount of agony of decision addressed to this subject in recent months has been out of proportion to what was actually involved.

Secondly, it may as well be recognized that the emotional overtones which this subject carries for much of American opinion, added to the unresolved differences among us over basic questions of political policy toward the bloc, make it idle for us to think that we can approach the problem of our own role in East-West trade on the basis of a cool and detached appraisal of national interest. One does not need to argue about just what the configurations of a policy so calculated would be. Whatever they would be, if they involved any appreciable liberalization of what we have been doing in recent years, they would at once become controversial, particularly in congressional opinion, to a degree that would militate greatly against their effectiveness. It is, in short, a matter in which we are simply incapable of acting at this time in any purely detached manner. For this, a calmer state of opinion would be necessary, and there would have to be a wider consensus on fundamental questions of policy. For the moment, therefore, anything in the way of a major relaxation of our export controls or extension of our commercial dealings with Russia and the bloc, has to be regarded as simply subjectively unfeasible. The Russians and the satellites will have to understand that if they have favorable chances at all for trade with the West, these chances do not lie in our direction—at least not until there is a marked and prolonged improvement in the political atmosphere.

On the other hand, it should, I think, be recognized that in view of the many variations in the way this problem presents itself to us—the differences, for example, between the considerations affecting trade with the Soviet Union and those affecting trade with the satellites, or between those prevailing in the case of Yugoslavia and those affecting trade with other Communist nations—it is not a problem which lends itself favorably to treatment by sweeping general determinations of policy, and particularly not in the form of legislative strictures. To deal in any way effectively with this problem, we need flexibility of approach —we need the ability to discriminate intelligently. Even a policy which is in essence one of denial or restriction of trade, should not be anchored in sweeping legislative injunctions which leave nobody—not even the legislative branch itself—in a position to make intelligent exceptions. It would be better to have a more restrictive and negative policy which rested on a firm understanding between congressional leaders and the Executive but left somebody free to use his head when it needed to be used, than to try to pursue more liberal policies against the background of a jealous congressional disposition to prescribe and limit their effects by legislative action.

When it comes to our attitude toward the trading policies of our associates in Western Europe, quite other considerations apply than do in the case of our own trade. Here, again, the best answer would seem to be: relax—but in the other direction. If at home the need is for a reduction of tension and controversy by accepting the internal compulsions that make it difficult for us to trade with the bloc, in the case of our European associates it is a question of accepting those external compulsions which make it difficult for them *not* to trade.

This is not to be taken as a suggestion that our European friends should be told that so far as we are concerned anything goes, and that there are no measures of prudence we would consider to be in order. There will still be need, of course, for agreement with them over the definition of what constitutes strategic materials, unsuitable for release to a politically hostile government. There may well be, as in the case of Soviet oil shipments, instances in which it will be necessary for us to take a sympathetic attitude toward, or even associate ourselves with, measures of collective defense, designed to prevent Western markets from being dangerously affected by Soviet trading practices. But whether we should try to bring pressure on the Western Europeans in matters of normal trade with the Communist bloc is another matter. They are not apt to agree entirely, no matter how hard we press, with those outlooks in this country which place such heavy limitations on our own ability to shape policy in this field. Their problems are in many respects their own, not ours. And we, divided and vacillating as we are in our basic judgments as to how to face the problem of international communism, are not apt to be very helpful guides to others in the shaping of their economic policies in the field of East-West trade.

Continued pressures on our European allies for the restriction of their trade with the Soviet Union and the bloc are unlikely to be very effective in hampering Soviet economic development. But there are two other effects they *are* likely to have. The first, which may be predicted with some confidence on the basis of past experience, is to place further strain on our relations with our European partners and to give us one more thing to disagree and argue about. The second is to throw just enough uncertainty into the minds of the Western Europeans to prevent them from doing anything very effective on their own in the way of giving Eastern Europe the alternative it needs, and to some extent is seeking, to an exclusive economic association with the Soviet bloc. To the extent that the Western Europeans are willing to move in the direction of expanded East-West trade, it would not seem to be our business to attempt to stop them, whatever our own feelings. For the opposite concept, the one which sees Russia's economic advance being importantly impeded by something like a Western blockade, is not going to work anyway beyond a point; and in moving to prevent the first one from being tried, even by our allies, we will simply be assuring that there can be no effective Western policy at all in this field: no effective policy of the denial of trade, because objective conditions do not permit it; no effective policy of its extension, because our pressures will be just sufficient to make it a half-hearted and half-way measure.

These are my reasons for suggesting that, while exercising in regard to our own trade with the . . . [Communists] whatever restraint is necessary to retain a reasonably adequate consensus of opinion behind our policy, we reduce the claims we place on the policies of our various allies and associates throughout the world, and leave them greater freedom to decide for themselves what they want to do. This will ease our relationship with them. It will permit us to satisfy our own pangs of conscience about trading with a political antagonist. The loss to be suffered, in terms of the pace of Russia's economic advance, will not be great, even in the eyes of those who see our purposes advanced only by Russia's economic setbacks. And meanwhile, we will at least permit to be conducted, to the extent our Western European friends have the inclination to conduct it, an experiment in which many of us may not greatly believe but which it is unnecessary and perhaps dangerous for us to inhibit: whether, namely, the possibility of better trading opportunities with the West—for Russia, the possibility of a better international division of labor in the interests of her own economic advance; for the satellites, the prospects of a reinclusion into the community of Europe in at least one important respect—whether this possibility will not have a useful effect on the Communist bloc as a whole, and produce such changes as to cause the entire problem of East-West trade to assume, eventually, a different and less forbidding aspect.

U.S. OBJECTIVES [6]

Whatever the causes, the process of change in Eastern Europe is bound to continue. The question facing all of us in the West is: How are we to deal with this development? What should be our policy objectives in Eastern Europe, and how are we to achieve them?

In formulating a policy, there are, I believe, several elements which we must keep in mind. When we use the phrase "Eastern Europe" we should stress the second word—"Europe." For after all, Eastern Europe is a part of Europe—a fact that is becoming

[6] From address, "Eastern Europe: A Region in Ferment," delivered by George C. McGhee, U.S. Ambassador to the Federal Republic of Germany, at symposium sponsored by the Youth Program of the City of Kassel and the America House, Kassel, Germany, October 13, 1964. *Department of State Bulletin.* 51:716-21. N. 16, '64.

increasingly apparent as the pattern of diversity, which the free West has never lost, begins once again to assert itself in the East.

Nor is the evolution toward conjunction with the West limited to gross appearances. The Eastern European nations want to do business with the West; their economic systems must perforce be adapted to an extent which will enable them to do so with some degree of efficiency. I do not suggest that the Marxists of Eastern Europe will become champions of free enterprise. Under the influence of commerce with the West, however, the economic institutions of Eastern Europe will inevitably become increasingly modified. . . .

Students of the Communist world have been much intrigued by . . . developments in Eastern Europe. Their assessment of the reasons for the changes there should be interesting for all of us. They conclude that one of the most likely causes for what has happened has been the monumental mismanagement by Marxist theoreticians of the economies of the various Eastern European Communist countries. Following years of economic troubles, in which governments failed to increase—in some instances, even to maintain—the material well-being of the population, popular resentment has exerted irresistible pressures for change.

The contrasting spectacle of economic dynamism and social progress in the free Western nations has exerted a profound influence. The swift postwar recovery and continuing rise of living standards in Western Europe—particularly in Germany—have had a magnetic effect on the people of Eastern Europe and their leaders. This is one of the reasons why there is an inevitable attraction of the Eastern states toward the West.

We must also acknowledge that Stalin's successors, some of whom fortunately did not fully share his relentless and brutal grasp of the mechanism of tyranny, found themselves unable to hold shut the gates against the floodtide of desire for change. They repudiated Stalin's bloody methods—though they were ready enough in Hungary in 1956 to use repression and bloodshed to stop an evolution which had become a revolution. However, the new wielders of Soviet power obviously foresaw that, if they were to have any hope at all of holding on in Eastern Europe, change was inevitable.

One factor which has undoubtedly played an important role is the example of Yugoslavia. That country's determination to assert its independence has encouraged those in other Eastern European nations who have followed the Soviet Union to feel their way, albeit in some cases cautiously, toward courses of action more in keeping with their own national interests.

Finally, I think we must inevitably conclude that the present rift between Communist China and the Soviet Union is a contributing factor toward change in Eastern Europe. As the two giants of the Communist world exchange insults and threats, the countries of Eastern Europe clearly feel increasing freedom of action. While maintaining its identity with communism—in most cases Soviet communism—each country tries to act as independently as it can within the limits of tolerance it feels it has. . . .

I am aware that there are those of the West who would like to erect a wall between the West and the whole Communist world—the effect of which would be to deliver Eastern Europe into Moscow's hands in perpetuity. These same people would have us follow one simple, basic policy toward all Communist countries. They would have us treat Albania as we would Poland, and vice versa.

The policy followed by my Government is far more complex and, I believe, far wiser. We are trying to encourage evolution within the Communist world toward national independence, peaceful cooperation. and open societies. We are trying to help promote a trend of developments in Eastern Europe which can, if advanced sufficiently, lead to ending the division of Europe and, as an inevitable corollary, the division of Germany. We believe that we can best promote these objectives by a flexible policy which takes account of the differing behavior of the various Communist countries—or the changing behavior of any one country. In our view, a rigid policy would not fit situations which in fact vary from country to country, nor would it be taken as a sign of strength by our adversaries. Our policy reflects, not weakness or indecisiveness, but the flexibility that can be afforded by those who are strong.

In all this there is nothing hostile to the Soviet Union—no intention to marshal the little European nations against the Soviets. I think we all recognize that these countries must have satisfactory and friendly relations with their giant neighbor to the East if they are to have any permanent sense of security. What I am advocating is the encouragement of conditions in Eastern Europe which would allow its member states to enter freely into relationships with both East and West—but under conditions determined by their own natural interests and not from coercion.

Specifically, American policy toward Eastern Europe has the following objectives:

(a) To see its peoples fully independent, prosperous, and restored to their natural and historic relationship with the rest of Europe and the free world. This concept is founded on our conviction that the achievement of self-determination in Eastern Europe, as everywhere, is essential to the establishment of a just and lastingly secure world order.

(b) To encourage a progressive loosening of external authority and control over the Eastern European countries and a continuation of the present trend to national autonomy and diversity. Such an evolution is a slow road but one which runs in the right direction—toward ultimate freedom and independence.

(c) To encourage developments which would enable the peoples of Eastern Europe to determine freely their own forms of government and to enjoy the fruits of national independence. This would contribute to the peace of Europe by leading to a more normal, stable, and healthy relationship between these people and their neighbors, including not just the West but the Soviet Union.

What, concretely, are the means the United States has adopted to carry out its policy toward the Eastern European states? In essence, we have shaped our actions to the differing requirements and opportunities of each case. In some instances initiatives to improve relations with the United States have come from the Eastern European countries themselves. We have welcomed and responded to them when there has been real evidence of a desire to better the state of affairs between us. In this connection it is significant that the jamming of the Voice of America in Eastern Europe has almost ceased. We have responded to the progress in Poland toward national independence by extending most-favored-nation treatment in trade and supplying agricultural products under Public Law 480.

Rumania's recent effort to expand its trade and other contacts with the West has included steps to improve relations with the United States. We are responding accordingly. In May of this year [1964] the United States and Rumania engaged in a comprehensive review of mutual relations and agreed on a number of specific measures to benefit trade and travel, as well as scientific and cultural exchanges between the two countries. We are watching developments closely in the other countries of Eastern Europe and will do what we can to encourage any tendencies to improve the lot of their people. [It was reported in January 1965 that the Rumanian government had signed preliminary contracts with American firms in the preceding month for the construction of a synthetic rubber plant and a petroleum cracking plant.—Ed.]

Let me stress again that what we see in Eastern Europe are trends—not a new world already in existence. Our policy by no means overlooks the tragic fact that these countries are still Communist-ruled. Americans have too many historic, personal, and cultural ties with Eastern Europe not to be sympathetically aware that there has as yet been no free expression of popular will in that area. There remain deep differences between the governments of Eastern Europe and the West. And insofar as these Communist governments remain committed to world revolution, our policy takes that fact, too into account.

This policy is formulated in the full knowledge that communism is a tyrant over peoples and a danger to the peace of the world. Yet it is formulated also in the belief—of which Eastern Europe has given concrete proof—that the domains over which communism rules are not inhabited by peoples in whom the desire for freedom is dead. These two truths dictate the course we follow, one of clear principle expressed in carefully graded actions. Communism's attempts to achieve greater power in the world, we oppose with all our strength. Movement toward national independence and greater liberty within nations in the Communist sphere we encourage with the peaceful means at our disposal.

This is not the easiest policy to pursue but is certainly the wisest. It requires a constant exercise of judgment, a careful weighing of actions which may appear superficially similar but have opposite results if applied in dissimilar circumstances. It is not a policy which lends itself to slogans. Its pursuit demands patience and unflagging attention to detail. If we persist in it, however, we shall find that the ferment in Eastern Europe will yield a new wine of hope in a vintage season that is approaching.

BIBLIOGRAPHY

An asterisk (*) preceding a reference indicates that the article or a part of it has been reprinted in this book.

BOOKS, PAMPHLETS, AND DOCUMENTS

Bain, L. B. Reluctant satellites: an eyewitness report on East Europe and the Hungarian revolution. Macmillan. New York. '60.

*Bass, Robert. Eastern Europe: a new orbit? (Headline Series no 168) Foreign Policy Association. 345 E. 46th St. New York, N.Y. 10017. D. 20, '64.

Betts, R. R. ed. Central and South-East Europe, 1945-1948. Royal Institute of International Affairs. London. '50.

Brzezinski, Z. K. The Soviet bloc: unity and conflict. Praeger. New York. '61.

Collier, D. S. and Glaser, Kurt, eds. Berlin and the future of Eastern Europe. Regnery. Chicago. '63.

Columbia University. Russian Institute. Anti-Stalin campaign and international communism. Columbia University Press. New York. '56.

Dallin, Alexander, ed. Diversity in international communism; a documentary record. Columbia University Press. New York. '63.

*Decter, Moshe. Profile of communism: a fact-by-fact primer. rev. ed. Collier Books. New York. '61.

Djilas, Milovan. New class. Praeger. New York. '57.

Fischer-Galati, Stephen, ed. Eastern Europe in the sixties. Praeger. New York. '63.

Fischer-Galati, Stephen. Romania. Praeger. New York. '57.

*Foreign Policy Association. Great decisions 1965. The Association. 345 E. 46th St. New York, N.Y. 10017. '65.

   Reprinted in this book: Fact Sheet no 2. Germany: sketch of a satellite. p 21; Fact sheet no 5. Eastern Europe: end of the satellite era? p 54-8.

Freidin, Seymour. Forgotten people. Scribner. New York. '62.

Griffith, W. E. Albania and the Sino-Soviet rift. M.I.T. Press. Cambridge, Mass. '63.

Halecki, Oscar. Borderlands of Western civilization: a history of East Central Europe. Ronald. New York. '52.

Halecki, Oscar, ed. East Central Europe under the Communists. Praeger. New York. '57.

Hamm, Harry. Albania: China's beachhead in Europe. Praeger. New York. '63.

*Hoffman, G. W. Balkans in transition. Van Nostrand. Princeton, N.J. '63.

*Isenberg, Irwin. Soviet satellites of Eastern Europe. Scholastic Magazines. New York. '63.

Judy, Richard. Communist agriculture—crisis and change. (Headline Series no 162) Foreign Policy Association. 345 E. 46th St. New York, N.Y. 10017. '63.

Kecskemeti, Paul. Unexpected revolution: social forces in the Hungarian uprising. Stanford University Press. Stanford, Calif. '61.

*Kennan, G. F. On dealing with the Communist world. Harper. New York. '64.

Kertesz, S. D. ed. East Central Europe and the world. University of Notre Dame Press. Notre Dame, Ind. '62.

Laqueur, W. Z. and Labedz, Leopold, eds. Polycentrism. Praeger. New York. '62.

Lasky, M. J. ed. Hungarian revolution. Praeger. New York. '57.

Lengyel, Emil. 1,000 years of Hungary. Day. New York. '58.

Macartney, C. A. Hungary: a short history. Aldine. Chicago. '62.

Mosely, P. E. ed. Kremlin and world politics. Vintage. New York. '60.

Pentony, D. E. ed. Red world in tumult: Communist foreign policies. Chandler. San Francisco. '62.

Pounds, N. J. G. Divided Germany and Berlin. Van Nostrand. Princeton, N.J. '62.

*Pounds, N. J. G. Poland between East and West. Van Nostrand. Princeton, N.J. '64.

Prittie, Terence. Germany divided. Little. Boston. '60.

Pryor, F. L. Communist foreign trade system. M.I.T. Press. Cambridge, Mass. '63.

Ripka, Hubert. Eastern Europe in the post-war world. Praeger. New York. '61.

Rothschild, Joseph. Communist Eastern Europe. Walker. New York. '64.

Rothschild, Joseph. Communist party of Bulgaria. Columbia University Press. New York. '59.

Seton-Watson, Hugh. East European revolution. Praeger. New York. '57.

Seton-Watson, Hugh. Eastern Europe between the wars, 1918-1941. Macmillan. New York. '46.

*Seton-Watson, Hugh. New imperialism. Dufour Editions. Chester Springs, Pa. '62.

Skendi, Stavro. Albania. Praeger. New York. '57.

Staar, R. F. Poland, 1944-1962: the Sovietization of a captive people. Louisiana State University Press. Baton Rouge. '62.

Steel, Ronald. End of alliance: America and the future of Europe. Viking. New York. '64.

Stillman, E. O. ed. Bitter harvest: the intellectual revolt behind the Iron Curtain. Praeger. New York. '59.

Taborsky, Edward. Communism in Czechoslovakia, 1948-1960. Princeton University Press. Princeton, N.J. '61.

Ulam, Adam. Titoism and the Cominform. Harvard University Press. Cambridge, Mass. '52.

*United Nations. General Assembly. Special Committee on the Problem of Hungary. Report. (Official Records, 11th session. Supplement no 18) United Nations. New York. '57.
    Also in New York Times. p 10-11. Je. 21, '57.

*United States. Senate. Committee on Foreign Relations. United States foreign policy: U.S.S.R. and Eastern Europe; a study prepared at the request of the Committee by a Columbia-Harvard research group. 86th Congress, 2d session. Supt. of Docs. Washington, D.C. 20402. '60.

*Urban, G. R. ed. Scaling the wall—talking to Eastern Europe; the best of Radio Free Europe. Wayne State University Press. Detroit. '64.
    Reprinted in this book: A patchwork quilt in Eastern Europe. J. F. Brown. p 185-91.

Vali, F. A. Rift and revolt in Hungary. Harvard University Press. Cambridge, Mass. '61.

Wolfers, Arnold, ed. Changing East-West relations and the unity of the West. Johns Hopkins. Baltimore. '64.

Wolff, R. L. Balkans in our time. Harvard University Press. Cambridge, Mass. '56.

Zinner, P. E. Communist strategy and tactics in Czechoslovakia, 1918-1948. Praeger. New York. '63.

Zinner, P. E. Revolution in Hungary. Columbia University Press. New York. '62.

PERIODICALS

General

See issues of East Europe *and* Journal of Central European Affairs.

America. 110:663. My. 16, '64. May Day troubles.

America. 112:18-20. Ja. 2, '65. New breed behind the Iron Curtain. G. J. Prpic.

Business Week. p 74+. N. 28, '64. Iron grip falters.

Christian Science Monitor. p 3. O. 7, '64. Communist collectives lag. Eric Bourne.

Christian Science Monitor. p 2. Ja. 18, '65. Comecon's soft spots. J. A. May.

Commonweal. 80:596-600. S. 4, '64. Kafka east, Kafka west. Harvey Cox.

Current History. 43:35-42. Jl. '62. Communist bloc in world trade. Milton Kovner.

Current History. 43:88-94+. Ag. '62. United States trade and the Soviet bloc. V. E. Mares.

*Current History. 44:257-320. My. '63. East Europe [entire issue].
  Reprinted in this book: Titoism in flux. F. W. Neal. p 294-8+.

Current History. 47:257-65. N. '64. After Khrushchev: what next? H. R. Swearer.

Current History. 47:272-9+. N. '64. East Europe's second chance. V. E. Mares.

Current History. Mr. '65. East Europe [entire issue].

Department of State Bulletin. 49:87-92. Jl. 15, '63. United States and Eastern Europe; address, June 14, 1963. Eugenie Anderson.

Department of State Bulletin. 50:390-6. Mr. 16, '64. Why we treat Communist countries differently; address, February 25, 1964. Dean Rusk.

Department of State Bulletin. 50:485-7. Mr. 30, '64. Conditions in Eastern Europe; statement, March 10, 1964. W. A. Harriman.

*Department of State Bulletin. 51:716-21. N. 16, '64. Eastern Europe: a region in ferment; address, October 13, 1964. G. C. McGhee.

Department of State Bulletin. 51:870-6. D. 21, '64. Dynamics of progress in central Europe; address, November 11, 1964. G. C. McGhee.

*East Europe. 13:3-9. Mr. '64. Comecon today. Michael Gamarnikow.

*East Europe. 13:11-15. My. '64. Future of Eastern Europe. George Mueller and others.

*Economist. 211:924-6. My. 30, '64. Johnson over Elbe.

Economist. 211:1215-16. Je. 13, '64. Twain shall meet.

Economist. 213:339-40+. O. 24, '64. October revolution; how Khrushchev fell.

Economist. 213:491-2. O. 31, '64. Communists march on Moscow [over abrupt removal of Mr. Khrushchev].

Foreign Affairs. 39:430-43. Ap. '61. Challenge of change in the Soviet bloc. Zbigniew Brzezinski.

Foreign Affairs. 42:171-83. Ja. '64. Polycentrism and Western policy. G. F. Kennan.

Foreign Affairs. 43:331-48. Ja. '65. Communist rule in Eastern Europe. J. M. Montias.

International Affairs (London). 39:1-12+. Ja. '63. Polish plan for a nuclear-free zone today. Adam Rapacki.

International Conciliation. 549:3-62. S. '64. Comecon. Andrzej Korbonski.

Life. 55:102-14. N. 15, '63. Faces of the satellites. Paul Schutzer.

Nation. 198:644-6. Je. 29, '64. Russia's Europe; shifting satellites. Alexander Werth.

Nation. 200:27-9. Ja. 11, '65. Russia's satellites in new orbit. Alexander Werth.

National Review. 11:413-15. D. 16, '61. Eastern Europe revisited. M. K. Dzjewanowski.

National Review. 16:111. F. 11, '64. Satellite blues. E. M. von Kuehnelt-Leddihn.

Nation's Business. 51:62-3. D. '63. Soviet empire will face new stresses. R. H. Davis.

Nation's Business. 52:34-5+. Je. '64. What Communist breakup means to us: interview with Zbigniew Brzezinski.

New Leader. 47:8-11. My. 25, '64. Now there are seven. Anatole Shub.

New Republic. 147:18-20. S. 17, '62. Common Market and Comecon. Alec Nove.

New Republic. 147:19-22. N. 3, '62. Report from the Red Riviera. Philip Ben.

New Republic. 148:18-20. Mr. 30, '63. Khrushchev's European allies. J. F. Brown.

New Republic. 150:8. My. 2, '64. East Europe: new directions.

New York Times. p 14. S. 17, '63. Soviet bloc in the 60's: comfort supplants fear as incentive. Max Frankel.

*New York Times. p 46. My. 24, '64. Text of speech by President Johnson, Lexington, Va., May 23, 1964.

*New York Times. p 1+. O. 21, '64. East Europe cold to changes in Soviet regime. H. E. Salisbury.

New York Times. p 1+, O. 26, '64. Profound change in Red bloc seen. A. J. Olsen.

*New York Times. p E7. N. 1, '64. East Europe asks: "What goes on in Moscow?" A. J. Olsen.

New York Times. p E3. N. 15, '64. Russia's satellites: diversity grows. Max Frankel.

New York Times. p E4. N. 29, '64. East Europe seeks 'bridges' to West. Max Frankel.

New York Times. p 1+. Ja. 11, '65. Talking tour of the Soviet bloc discloses bitterness and hope. Max Frankel.

New York Times. p 1+. Ja. 14, '65. East bloc 20 years after war: wealth, stability still elude it. Max Frankel.

New York Times. p 65. Ja. 15, '65. Communist countries discarding the grinding gears of centralized management. David Binder.

New York Times. p 10. Ja. 18, '65. Changes in Eastern Europe: a country by country report. Max Frankel.

New York Times Magazine. p 9+. Ap. 26, '59. Forgotten clue to central Europe. A. M. Rosenthal.

New York Times Magazine. p 22-3+. Mr. 15, '64. Moscow's satellites; in and out of orbit. Anatole Shub.

New York Times Magazine. p 28+. Ap. 19, '64. Jokes that seep through the Iron Curtain. Peggy Streit.

New York Times Magazine. p 14-15+. My. 24, '64. Tough time for puritans behind the Iron Curtain. Cynthia Grenier.

New York Times Magazine. p 32-3+. N. 29, '64. Don't underestimate Europe. J. C. Harsch.

Newsweek. 62:36-8+. O. 28, '63. World in change: a trip through Eastern Europe. Eldon Griffiths.

Same abridged: Reader's Digest. 84:119-24. Ap. '64.

Newsweek. 63:34+. F. 10, '64. Creeping together: U.S.-Soviet bloc relations.

Newsweek. 63:47-8+. Ap. 27, '64. Splintered legacy of Karl Marx.

Newsweek. 64:35-6. Ag. 10, '64. Crumbling of ideology. R. S. Elegant.

*Problems of Communism. 13:73-81. Mr.-Ap. '64. Perspectives for Eastern Europe. R. V. Burks.

Reporter. 27:27-30. Jl. 19, '62. Communist dread of the Common Market. Madeleine Kalb and Marvin Kalb.

Reporter. 30:29-31. Ja. 2, '64. Winter of communism's discontent. Anatole Shub.

Saturday Evening Post. 232:13-15+. Ja. 30; 24-5+. F. 6; 40-1+. F. 13, '60. I saw what makes communism work. Stewart Alsop.

    Same abridged with title: What I saw in Khrushchev's uneasy empire. Reader's Digest. 76:53-9. My. '60.

Saturday Evening Post. 236:23-9, 88. O. 12, '63. Khrushchev's hidden weakness; captive nations. R. M. Nixon.

    Same abridged: Reader's Digest. 84:59-64. Ja. '64.

Saturday Evening Post. 237:13. N. 21, '64. Moscow: which way? Stewart Alsop.

Saturday Review. 44:13-15. Jl. 15, '61. Mood inside Russia's satellites. Louis Fischer.

Senior Scholastic. 82:11-16. F. 6. '63. European Red empire. G. L. Steibel.

Time. 84:112. O. 2, '64. New managers: discovering capitalism in the Soviet bloc.

Travel. 120:47-51. Jl. '63. Down the Danube. Mary Elsy.

U.S. News & World Report. 51:67-8+. S. 25, '61. Red blight on the Balkans. F. B. Stevens.

U.S. News & World Report. 54:45-7. My. 6, '63. No boom in the Red empire.

U.S. News & World Report. 56:48-54. Ap. 20, '64. Is Russia losing East Europe? Charles Foltz, Jr.

U.S. News & World Report. 57:79-81. O. 5, '64. Cracks in Russia's empire.

Albania

Atlantic. 211:41-50. Je. '63. Albania: the last Marxist paradise. James Cameron.

*Christian Science Monitor. p 1+. N. 12, '64. Albanian Reds as stern
as ever. G. M. Panarity.

Foreign Affairs. 40:471-8. Ap. '62. Albania and the Sino-Soviet conflict.
Stravro Skendi.

New Republic. 148:11-14. Ja. 26, '63. Albania and her neighbors. W. E.
Griffith.

Reporter. 25:29-30. N. 23, '61. Pawn on the Adriatic. I. R. Levine

Saturday Evening Post. 235:17-23. Mr. 17, '62. Albania: where Stalin
still rules. Harry Hamm.

Time. 84:46. D. 11, '64. Independent dummy.

Bulgaria

*New York Times. p 25. S. 20, '64. Bulgaria trying new directions.
David Binder.

Time. 84:26-7. S. 25, '64. Life of a lap dog.

Travel. 115:42-6. My. '61. Bulgaria. Don Fitzgerald.

Czechoslovakia

Atlantic. 214:12+. N. '64. Atlantic report: Czechoslovakia.

Atlantic. 215:100-4+. F. '65. Footloose in Prague: a Marxist Bohemia.
Curtis Cate.

Economist. 213:953-5. N. 28, '64. No defenestration today [report on
Czechoslovakia].

Encounter. 23:27-34. S. '64. Prague: a visa for Kafka. Goronwy Rees.

Foreign Affars. 42:320-8. Ja. '64. Czech Stalinists die hard. V. A.
Velen.

Nation. 199:171-2. S. 28, '64. Letter from Prague. Robert Littell.

New Republic. 151:7-8. D. 12, '64. Reform yes, revolution no. Max
Frankel.

*New York Times. p 1+. N. 6, '64. Czechs revamping economic system.
Max Frankel.

Newsweek. 63:48+. My. 18, '64. No time for jokes.

Newsweek. 64:52+. D. 7, '64. Czechoslovakia: the gymnast. Kenneth
Ames.

Problems of Communism. 13:4-14. My.-Je. '64. Czechoslovakia: out of
Stalinism? Edward Taborsky.

*Reporter. 30:15-20. My. 7, '64. Kafka's nightmare comes true. George Bailey.

Travel. 115:37-41. My. '61. Czechoslovakia. Veronica Weir.

East Germany

Atlantic. 212:114-17. D. '63. What Ulbricht doesn't know. Kurt Wismach.

Economist. 211:125-6. Ap. 11, '64. East Germany; notes from beyond the Elbe.

Economist. 212:902+. S. 5, '64. Divided Germany; unrecognisable Ulbricht?

Encounter. 23:40-7. S. '64. Berlin: beyond the wall. John Mander.

International Affairs (London). 39:59-73. Ja. '63. Berlin crisis 1958-1962. Elisabeth Barker.

Nation. 199:84-5. S. 7, '64. Booty at the back door. Max Madden.

New Republic. 147:13-16. Jl. 9, '62. What is at stake in Berlin? L. J. Halle.

New York Herald Tribune. p 1. O. 4, '64. East Germany's 15th year: a trifle of liberalization. Myron Kandel.

New York Times Magazine. p 27+. Mr. 25, '62. Why Ulbricht keeps his job. Flora Lewis.

New York Times Magazine. p 36+. Ap. 8, '62. Journey to the silent Germany. Robert Alden.

Newsweek. 61:42+. F. 18, '63. Inside Ulbricht's empire; with report by R. S. Elegant.

*Newsweek. 64:46-7. N. 23, '64. East Germany: quiet revival. Kenneth Ames.

Problems of Communism. 12:1-14. Jl.-Ag. '63. East Germany today: The persistence of Stalinism. Martin Janicke; Notes on a somber journey. Erich Balow.

Time. 83:26. Je. 19, '64. Sop for Walter; friendship pact between East Germany and the Soviet Union.

U.S. News & World Report. 57:84. Ag. 17, '64. Reds' pet satellite looks west.

Hungary

Atlas. 7:216-19. Ap. '64. What makes Hungary tick? Willy Linder.

Economist. 208:1106+. S. 28, '63. Looking out from Central Europe; Hungary in the shallows.

Encounter. 23:35-9. S. '64. Budapest: alien's return. George Mikes.

New Republic. 150:7. F. 15, '64. New Hungary. Philip Ben.

New York Times Magazine. p 6-7+. D. 27, '64. 10,000,000 Hungarians can't be wrong. David Binder.

New Yorker. 40:121-2+. Mr. 14, '64. Letter from Budapest. Joseph Wechsberg.

Newsweek. 64:39-40. Jl. 27, '64. Hungary: the new aristocracy.

Problems of Communism. 13:24-34. My.-Je. '64. Hungary: literary renascence. L. M. Tikos.

Saturday Evening Post. 234:25+. F. 25, '61. Submission of Hungary. F. O. Hauser.

*Saturday Evening Post. 237:38+. Ap. 25, '64. Hungary: renaissance after revolt. David Holden.

Poland

America. 111:397. O. 10, '64. Tolerant Polish Reds.

Business Week. p 190-2+. N. 16, '63. Slumping between two worlds.

Commentary. 35:210-19. Mr. '63. Polish miracle. R. H. S. Crossman.

Commonweal. 80:228-32. My. 15, '64. Polish paradox. T. D. Langan.

Current History. 36:205-9+. Ap. '59. Poland: geography for disaster. H. H. Kostanick.

*East Europe. 13:30-3. Je. '64. Poland's unemployment problem. Michael Gamarnikow.

*East Europe. 13:34-7. Je. '64. Affair of the Polish intellectuals.

Foreign Affairs. 40:635-43. Jl. '62. Nationalism and communism in Poland. Adam Bromke.

*Listener. 72:577-9. O. 15, '64. Warsaw rising. Zbigniew Pelczynski.

National Review. 16:809-12. S. 22, '64. Personal observations from abroad: free and less free; red tape in Warsaw. P. L. Buckley.

New Leader. 47:4-7. My. 11, '64. Myth of Polish liberalism. Andrew Field.

New Republic. 149:10. Jl. 13, '63. Poland. W. Z. Laqueur.

New Republic. 151:15-18. O. 3, '64. Walk through Warsaw. L. J. Halle.
    Reply: 151:38. N. 14, '64. J. Jedruch.

New York Times. p 1+. N. 15, '64. Poland is troubled by growing unrest. Max Frankel.

New York Times Magazine. p 24+. S. 13, '59. To understand Poland, understand Gomulka. A. M. Rosenthal.

New York Times Magazine. p 36-7+. Mr. 5, '61. Poland today, a poeple's paradox. A. J. Olsen.

New Yorker. 38:106+. F. 9, '63. Letter from Warsaw. Joseph Wechsberg.

Reporter. 30:9-10. My. 7, '64. It happened in Poland; restrictions on allocations of paper for printing of books and periodicals.

Senior Scholastic. 77:12-15+. Ja. 11, '61. Poland: crack in the Iron Curtain.

Rumania

Business Week. p 154+. My. 16, '64. Satellite veers off course.

Christian Science Monitor. p 1. My. 15, '64. Washington tries Rumanian yardstick. R. R. Brunn.

Commonweal. 81:10-12. S. 25, '64. Rumania looks west. M. M. Mestrovic.

*Economist. 212:1119-20+. S. 19, '64. Rumanian recipe; special report.

Newsweek. 63:74. Je. 15, '64. Shopping list; U.S. and Rumanian economic pact.

Newsweek. 64:31-5. Ag. 10, '64. Satellite looks west.

Problems of Communism. 13:14-19+. My.-Je. '64. Rumania: onto the separate path. R. L. Braham.

Reporter. 31:33-4. N. 5, '64. A place to sleep in Rumania. George Bailey.

*Reporter. 31:25-30. N. 19, '64. Trouble over Transylvania. George Bailey.

Saturday Review. 46:18-19. Jl. 13, '63. Rolling out a red Carpathian. Horace Sutton.

Senior Scholastic. 85:14-16+. O. 28, '64. Rumania: satellite out of orbit?

Time. 84:31. Jl. 24, '64. Independent satellite.

U.S. News & World Report. 57:22. Jl. 20, '64. Rumania's Gheorghiu-Dej; another rebel Red?

Yugoslavia

Atlantic. 210:73-128+. D. '62. Yugoslavia; symposium.

*Christian Science Monitor. p 1. S. 4, '64. Belgrade remaps agriculture. Eric Bourne.

Commonweal. 77:402-3. Ja. 11, '63. Tito's return to Moscow. M. M. Mestrovic.

Commonweal. 80:542-4. Ag. 7, '64. My friend, the Titoist. Adolph Schalk.

Economist. 207:756. My. 25, '63. Marxist front; Tito's contribution.

Foreign Affairs. 41:384-97. Ja. '63. Jugoslavia: crisis and choice. J. C. Campbell.

Fortune. 63:98+. Je. '61. Tito's westward tack.

Harper's Magazine. 223:11-15. Ag. '61. Yugoslavia's flirtation with free enterprise. John Fischer.

International Commerce. 70:8-9. My. 25, '64. Yugoslav economy; expensive food for thought.

National Geographic Magazine. 121:218-47. F. '62. Yugoslavia's window on the Adriatic. G. M. Grosvenor.

New Leader. 46:3-5. S. 16. '63. 'Pas de deux' in the Balkans: Khrushchev and Tito. Anatole Shub.

New York Times Magazine. p 24+. O. 13, '63. Active coexister visits us. David Binder.

Saturday Evening Post. 236:75-9. Je. 22, '63. How well can we trust Marshal Tito? Robert Sherrod.

Senior Scholastic. 83:12-15+. O. 11, '63. Tito of Yugoslavia: new role for an old rebel?

World Politics. 16:418-41. Ap. '64. Yugoslav commune. J. C. Fisher.

Yale Review. 53:221-32. D. '63. Yugoslavia: after the Partisan generation. Abraham Rothberg.